KOREAN-AMERICAN WOMEN:
toward self-realization

Edited

by

Inn Sook Lee

WIPF & STOCK · Eugene, Oregon

Wipf and Stock Publishers
199 W 8th Ave, Suite 3
Eugene, OR 97401

Korean American Women
Toward Self-Realization
By Lee, Inn Sook
Copyright© by Lee, Inn Sook
ISBN 13: 978-1-60608-545-5
Publication date 2/11/2009
Previously published by The Association of
Korean Christian Scholars in North America, Inc., 1985

to

Our foremothers
Who pioneered our path
in this land, and

to

Korean-American women of future generations
who will follow their footsteps
in different ways

CONTENTS

CONTRIBUTORS

MINZA KIM BOO is a doctoral candidate in the Department of Sociology at West Virginia University, and her M.S.W. degree is from Howard University in Washington D.C. She served on the Board of Directors of AKCS and is the Director of The Council of International Program for Youth Leaders and Social Workers at West Virginia University.

BEVERLY W. HARRISON is Professor of Christian Ethics at Union Theological Seminary in New York, and she earned her Ph.D. from Union Theological Seminary. She is the author of *Right to Choose and Making the Connections: Essays in Feminist Social Ethics.* She is active serving as a resource person in the areas of church and society and women's concerns for the Presbyterian Church (U.S.A.)

WON MOO HURH is Professor in the Department of Sociology and Anthropology at Western Illinois University in Macomb. He received his Ph.D. from Heidelberg University in Germany. He has done extensive research on Korean Immigrants in urban areas, and his publications include "Toward A New Community and Identity: The Korean-American Ethnicity" included in *The Korean Immigrant in American* (Kim and Lee, eds., AKCS, 1980.)

KWANG CHUNG KIM is Professor in the Department of Sociology and Anthropology at Western Illinois University in Macomb. His Ph.D. is from Indiana University. He has published many articles on Korean Immigrants in urban areas, and one of them is entitled "Intra-and inter-group conflicts: The Case of Korean Small Business in the United States," which was included in the book *Korean Women* (Sunoo and Kim, eds., AKCS, 1978.)

DANIEL B. LEE is Professor in the Department of Sociology at Ohio State University in Columbus, and his D.S.W. is from University of Utah. He is the founder and Director of The Transcultural Family Institute, Inc., and is active in training the helping professionals in counseling the transcultural families.

INN SOOK LEE is Ed.D. candidate in the Department of Philosophy and Social Sciences at Columbia University in New York city, and her M.A. degree is from Columbia University. She will be teaching at New York Theological Seminary as Professor of Pastoral Theology and serving as the Director of Asian American Programs. She was a staff in Program Agency in Presbyterian Church (USA), and is active in National Korean Presbyterian Women. She served as the first woman General Secretary of AKCS.

LETTY M. RUSSELL is Professor of the Practice of Theology at Yale Divinity School, and earned her doctorate from Union Theological Seminary in New York. She is an ordained Presbyterian minister and served as pastor and educator in the East Harlem Protestant Parish for seventeen years. Her publications include *Growth in Partnership* and *Becoming Human* and she serves on various Committees of the National Council of Churches and the World Council of Churches.

Introduction

Reserved, submissive, passive—these are the images of Koean-American women held by many. They are the characteristics derived from the Asian cultural tradition of the past. But I have witnessed the persistent, undying inner-strength and power of perseverance working in the core of their existence.

Based on this unspoken strength, we need to work toward attaining a consciousness for our potential for self-realization and authentic full humanity. This struggle is based on our belief that we are created in the image of God. We have been created to live, to share and to love as free human beings.

Since the pervasive images are passive, submissive and self-sacrificing, the Korean-American women's struggle for a positive self-identity and self-realization is not easy. The internalized self-image of passivity as femininity held by Korean women is hard to overcome.

Racial-ethnic women in this society are the victims of a multilayered oppression. They are suffering from a sense of invisibility and negation relegated from racism and sexism prevailing in the American society.

Korean-American women are oppressed even further. A young kindergartener would go to school on her first day of school, and is surrounded by others. She is asked, "Are you Chinese or Japanese?". "Neither!" she replies shyly. She is bluntly asked again, "What are you, then?". The sense of invisibility and non-recognition even among Asians is deeply felt.

Korean women began to immigrate to the United States at the turn of the century. Over 7,000 Korean men arrived at Hawaiian Isalnds during early 1900s' to work as laborers at Sugar Plantations. Many women came as "picture brides" and worked alongside their husbands at the plantation, and later at the farm as well as at home fulfilling domestic duties, raising and educating their children (Sunoo, AKCS Series #2, 1977). Women held lower status at home, and they worked hard mostly to cater to the needs of their husbands and other members of the family.

The ingenuity and perseverance they had demonstrated under those hardships provide a powerful and enduring example to follow for Korean-American women today. Many of them made significant contributions to Korean immigrant church and communities, as well as to their family life.

Korean-American women live with an unconscious self-image of traditional women who suffered under oppressive cultural system for many years. In addition, contemporary Korean-American women live feeling caught in-between the two cultures. they feel they should follow the traditional expectations on the one hand, and the newly acquired westernized contemporary modes, on the other. They feel they should assert their individual rights and also restrain the same, feeling an acute contradiction within themselves. Eastern culture demands modesty, obedience, conformity, obligation, family relationships, while western culture encourages individualism, assertiveness, materialism, and personal achievement.

The second and third generation struggle feeling caught between the two ideologies with strong emotional ties with parents, at the same time longing for self-assertion as individuals. They seem to establish strong self-identity after periods of painful struggle between complete assimilation in the white society and the deep immersion in thier own heritage.

Soon they seem to succeed in balancing value systems for themselves becoming independent individuals, at the same time maintaining warm relationships with family members. They are known for tolerance for diverse cultural elements, adaptability to new situations, and almost a complete absence of prejudice.

Many first generation Korean-American women feel left out in family situations, neither able to communicate with their children on the satisfactory level nor able to help them with their home work due to the language and cultural differences. They experience the loss of cultural pride, identity crisis, social marginality and subtle yet existing discrimination and invisibility in society.

In spite of a sense of isolation suffered by Korean-

American Women, much strength and ingenuity prevail. A large percentage of college graduates work in factories, shops and dry-cleaners, but developing themselves as good managers. Others work in offices and at home becoming professionals and social service workers.

Though in the process of becoming, many women feel critical need to be freed from the cultural and societal oppression. In light of the much sought after need, we present this volume, hoping to make a small contribution toward that immense task. The two articles included depict the strength of Korean women found in the life of immigrant community. The two essays are written with the hope of providing some insights and encouragement as we are engaged in the struggle to become whole and free human beings. The remaining two articles suggest critically important guidelines and distinctive vision for the work of self-realization of women.

The first article written by Professor Kwang Chung Kim and Professor Won Moo Hurh is based on their empirical research on the family roles among those who are engaged in small business in the south side of Chicago, depicting much strength and contribution made by women for family business as well as family life. Professor Lee's essay depicts much strength and contribution made by transculturally married women. No words can adequately describe the struggle and pain which the interacially married Korean women encounter day to day bases. The suffering they sustain from a sense of isolation and emotional turmoil derived from the lack of compassion and understanding by the people around them is great. In that situation, they have successfully managed even to help students, immigrant churches, and many Korean-American businesses.

The essay written by Ms. Minza Kim Boo is a timely and provocative essay much needed by Korean-American women, and provides an insight in their conflict-ridden emotional and social reality. This essay is the result of an in-depth and substantive research, and will make a profound contribution for Korean-American women in their struggle for self-understanding and self-realization. Professor Russell's essay is a brief but incisive critique for the renewal and mission of the church, expressing solidarity with women, and calling for a contextual theology. She asserts that only a theological reflection rooted in concrete cultural and social struggle of a group of people can express God's presence and solidarity with those people.

Ms. Inn Sook Lee's article is an overview of the feminist movement in contemporary Christian context, highlighting struggles for consciousness, human freedom and dignity, and calling for a just and supportive egalitarian Christian community. Professor Harrison's article is an important essay in the field of feminist moral theology. Her essay suggests the direction and guidance for those who are working toward conscientized and self-actualized selves, and working toward building a community of radical love based on the ideology of mutuality and reciprocity. She asserts that our power to rage against the evil that have been done, can and should be used as the root of the power for the radical work of love, helping us dedicate ourselves as the agents of love, in building the world with "no excluded ones" where dignity, respect and care for humanity prevail.

We are deeply grateful for the exhilarating experience of joint efforts rendered in the making of the present volume. This volume is the result of unceasing efforts given by many people for many months. We are also greatly indebted to the church agencies whose support made this publication possible. This particular issue was funded by the Women's Opportunity Giving of the Women's Program in the Presbyterian Church (U.S.A) and by the Office of Asian Mission Development in the Racial Justice division of the Program Agency, Presbyterian Church (U.S.A.)

We deeply appreciate the contributions made by the authors. We are especially grateful to Prof. Russell and Prof. Harrison for their unconditional support and encouragement for this publication. Our thanks are due to Mr. Cy Suh Hyong Lee and Dr. Lester Ruiz for reading the manuscripts. Mr. Dae Bok Kim rendered his expertise in cover and book design and we are also thankful for this courtesy and helpfulness. I am also grateful to the president Steve Rhew of AKCS, its former-president Sung Koog Hahm, and the entire Board of Directors for their support and patience.

Last but not the least I am indebted to Professor Sang Hyun Lee of Princeton Theological Seminary for his critically important friendship, sustaining support, and ongoing creative conversation rendered for this volume.

November, 1985
Princeton Junction, NJ   Inn Sook Lee

The Wives of Korean Small Businessmen in the U.S.: Business Involvement and Family Roles

Kwang Chung Kim
Won Moo Hurh

1. Introduction

Since the revision of the U.S. immigration law in 1965, the number of immigrants from Asian countries has been sharply increased (Bryce-Laporte, 1980). As a part of such immigration flow, a large number of Koreans have recently immigrated to the United States (Hurh and Kim, 1984: Ch. 2). The 1980 U.S. census showed that the number of Koreans in the United States reached 350,000. As one of the fastest growing immigrant groups, approximately 30,000 Koreans annually immigrate to the United States. If this trend continues, their number will double within the next decade.

Like other recent immigrant groups in the U.S., a high proportion of Korean immigrants are found to be actively engaged in self-employed small business (Bonacich, Light and Wong, 1980; Light, 1980; Hurh and Kim, 1984: Ch. 4; Hyung-Chan Kim, 1977; Ill Soo Kim, 1981: Ch. 4; Lovell-Troy, 1980; Wilson and Martin, 1982; Wilson and Portes, 1980; Waldinger,

1

1983). Bonacich, Light and Wong (1980) estimate that one quarter of Korean labor force in the Los Angeles area are in small business for themselves. Our recent study in the same area (1984) indicates that one third of the adult Korean immigrants are currently owners and/or managers of small business. This observation suggests that in order to understand the adjustment of Koreans and other recent immigrants in the U.S., it is necessary to examine their small business-related experiences. Waldinger expresses the importance of small business among the recent immigrant groups as follows:

Research on the new immigration has focused either on immigrant professionals entering high-level positions or on unskilled immigrant workers drawn into low-wage jobs in the secondary labor market. Yet there is a growing evidence that ethnic sub-economies made up of small, immigrant-owned and staffed businesses compromise a third increasingly important mode of occupational integration (1983:1).

A review of Korean small businesses reveals a number of interesting facts. First, Korean small businesses are highly concentrated in two labor-intensive industries: retail trade and services (Bonacich and Jung, 1982; Ill Soo Kim, 1981). Second, the scale of their business operation is very small even as compared with other small business establishments in the United States (Bonacich, Light and Wong, 1980; Jin, 1978; Hyung-Chan Kim, 1977; Kim and Wong, 1977). Korean small businesses can, therefore, be generally characterized as "small" small business or family small business (The State of Small Business, 1982: Table 1.6). Third, in terms of the ethnicity of their major customers (numerical majority), however, the markets of Korean small businesses are highly diversified which go beyond the "sheltered" or "protected" market of their own ethnic community. Bonacich and Jung (1982) note that three-fourths of Korean retail establishments in the Los Angeles area are located outside Korea-Town, and they are concentrated mainly in the underprivileged markets of other minority communities (e.g., blacks, Mexicans). These communities are characterized by a high rate of poverty, unemployment, crime and other socioeconomic hardships. Many Korean retail establishments are also located in the downtown areas of the major cities. Some are even located in the suburban areas or white neighborhoods. In short, the Korean small businesses in the United States are small, labor-intensive, and diversified in terms of the nature of their markets.

When the business scale is small, it is very important to examine the interpersonal contact that the business owners maintain with their significant others such as their family members, friends, kin, customers, suppliers, employees and so on. Such contact could involve considerable non-contractual elements through which the business owners obtain various types of support valuable to their business preparation and operation. In their study of the small businesses of the pre-war Japanese immigrants, Bonacich and Modell stress this point: "notably in marginal field of endeavor, non-contractual relations can be less expensive and more efficient than formal contractual ones as long as there remain less-developed niches within capitalistic society" (1980: 253). Unfortunately, study of the non-contractual support involved in minority-owned small businesses has been neglected.

As part of such non-contractual support, it is reported that Korean business owners have received a variety of support from their family members, friends and other members of their own ethnic group. Several scholars consider Korean immigrant entrepreneurs' effective utilization of such support as one of the most important factors for their business expansion (Bonacich, Jung, 1982; Bonacich, Light and Wong, 1980; Light, 1980).

In this context, this research concerns the non-contractual support that Korean entrepreneurs receive from their family members. Business involvement of family members as unpaid workers will cut down the labor cost of Korean small businesses and this inexpensive (cheap) form of labor will give Korean small businesses a decisive advantage to win business competition (Bonacich, 1978; Bonacich and Jung, 1982; Bonacich, Light and Wong, 1980). For this reason, Korean small businesses are generally expected to exhibit a high degree of absorptiveness.[1]

It is, however, observed that among family mem-

4

bers, the wife alone generally participates in the business activities (Hurh and Kim, 1984: Ch. 6). Most of the children in the Korean entrepreneurial families are either too young to work or are in school. Under this condition, the wife in the Korean entrepreneurs' families is virtually the only steady source of the unpaid family labor. This research will, therefore, mainly examine business involvement of the wives in the Korean entrepreneurs' families. For the study of their business involvement, however, it is necessary to consider the traditional marital roles dominant in Korea. We will review these traditional marital roles and some questions related to the adjustment of such roles among the Korean entrepreneurs' families in the next section.

2. Theoretical Framework

Based on the Confucian philosophy, Korean family system has traditionally provided a well-defined set of marital roles. The husband is expected to be

---

[1] Kanter defines the absorptiveness as "occupational pursuits that not only demand the maximum commitment of the workers and define the context for family life; but also implicate other family members and command their direct participation in the work system in either its formal or informal aspects" (1977: 26).

the provider for his family, while the wife expected to stay home and to serve devotedly her husband and other members of her husband's family (Choi Jai-Seuk, 1977: 8; Lee Hyo-Chae, 1973: 22). Under this system, a Korean married woman is confined to the home maker's role. These traditional marital roles have persisted in Korea in spite of the rapid industrialization that has taken place during the past two decades (Choi Jai-Seuk, 1977; Kim Haeng-Ja, 1978; Kim Hyon-Ja, 1971; Lee Hyo-Chae, 1973; Lee Hyo-Chae, 1973; Lee Hyo-Chae and Cho Hyoung, 1977).

The traditional marital roles are carried over to the U.S., and it is the responsibility of Korean immigrant husbands to support their families (Hurh and Kim, 1984: Ch. 6). When the immigrant husbands struggle hard to secure an economic base for their families, however, they often find themselves seriously disadvantaged in the American labor market due to language and other cultural problems, unfamiliarity with the American socioeconomic system, inferior educational credentialism, underemployment, discrimination and so on (Hurh and Kim, 1984: Ch. 6; Light, 1980). Such disadvantaged conditions turn the immigrant husbands into self-employed small business.

It is not, however, easy for immigrants or any other minority members to open a small business and to manage it successfully. They are severely handicapped by a number of problems, including those of limited managerial ability and experience, poor financing, limited access to business-related information, poor marketing, and discrimination and prejudice on the part of white businessmen (Doctors and Huff, 1973; Ch. 1; Fleming, 1979; Ledvinka and Pearson, 1971; MBDA Research Division, 1982; Ill Soo Kim, 1981; Ch. 4). Under these adverse circumstances, most of the immigrant husbands have to work extremely hard and mobilize family resources for business preparation and operation. This situation forces their wives to be involved in the business activities in various ways.

We will analyze the business involvement of these wives in terms of their work-family role adjustment. Family may be considered as both emotional and task units. As a task unit, family has to perform a number of tasks for the maintenance of the whole family and welfare of individual family members. Two types of such tasks are to secure material resources for family support and to perform household tasks such as dishwashing, laundry, grocery shopping and so on. In the industrialized society, securing material resources usually requires one to be employed outside the home, while performance of household tasks generally requires one to stay home and do daily chores. A crucial issue for the family as a task unit is who performs what tasks and to what extent among married couples.

For the analysis of such issue, Pleck (1977) offers a useful conceptual framework, the work-family role system. According to Pleck, the role system consists of the following four types of roles: (1) the male work role, (2) the male family role, (3) the female work role, and (4) the female family role. Based on this set of roles, he then proposes to pursue the following two points: (1) how married couples divide the work-family roles, and (2) how each of the work-family roles articulates with the others to which it is linked (1977; 417).

The main purpose of this research is to explore the work and family experiences of Korean immigrant entrepreneurs and their wives based on the above work-family role system. For this purpose, we may ask two crucial questions related to the work role of the immigrant wives: (1) To what extent are the wives involved in the business preparation and operation? (2) What kinds of contributions do the wives make at each stage of their business activities? We may then ask the following two questions related to the family role of the wives and their husbands: (1) When wives are involved in the business activities, will their work role reduce their family role? (2) Under this condition, will their husbands increase their family role? As an exploratory study, this research will prove these four questions.

In the study of immigrant small business, an important factor to be considered is the types of business opportunity available to the immigrants. This will influence the type of business that they run and the nature of their wives' business involvement. This opportunity factor is particularly important for Korean small business entrepreneurs who generally run retail or service businesses in the highly diversified markets.

It has been stated that the business expansion of Korean immigrants comes from their penetration into the markets of other minority communities. As a result of such penetration, a high proportion of the current Korean small businesses are currently located in the minority markets. In light of such market structure of Korean small businesses, this research will exclusively focus on the work-family role experiences of Korean immigrants who currently operate their business in the minority markets.

3. Data Collection

Data for this research were collected through interviewing 100 Korean immigrants who currently own small business and take the major responsibility of operating the business daily. These immigrant entrepreneurs were interviewed by four Korean interviewers using a standardized interview schedule from mid-January to the end of February, 1983.

Our respondents were selected on the basis of (1) the location of their current stores, and (2) their availability to this research. The Korean Chamber of Commerce in the Chicago area originally provided a list of 100 Korean small business owners who maintained their business in the south side of Chicago, the area of a heavy black concentration. Three fourths of our respondents were identified from this list and subsequently interviewed. The remaining one fourth were, however, not available to this research due to incorrect addresses, refusals and other circumstances. Under this condition, most of the remaining one-fourth of our respondents were selected, whenever our interviewers could physically locate the stores of Korean immigrants in the south side of Chicago and managed to interview them. Few of our respondents were, however, selected from those whose stores were located in other minority areas of Chicago.

Through the above procedure, we interviewed 100 Korean small business owners. Six of them were, however, eliminated due to the fact that the majority of their customers were not minority members. The analysis of this research is then based on the interview data from a total of 94 Korean small business owners.*

As expected, most of our respondents are males (84, 89.4%). The female owners (10, 10.6%) are generally in some unusual situations. Four of them are post-marital singles: the widowed, divorced or separated. One female owner lives in the Chicago south with her black husband and runs a small business. Other female owners manage their businesses because their husbands are employed

---

*Eighty four of the respondents specify the zip code of their current stores. Most of the stores of these respondents are found to be located in the following eight zip code areas: 60607 (10), 60609 (6), 60617 (10), 60619 (5), 60620 (6), 60623 (7), 60624 (16), 60628 (10).

elsewhere or run other businesses.

On the average, our respondents are 39.8 years old (SD=7.60) and their age ranges from 21 to 50. Most of the respondents (85, 90.4%) are married and live with their families. Most of these married respondents (79, 92.9%) have children and their children are generally young. Only 18 respondents indicate that their children are old enough (16 or older) to help their family business. Most of the married respondents (62, 72.9%) maintain the nuclear family. The remaining married respondents show that in addition to their own nuclear family members, they live with their or their spouses' parents (particularly mothers), sisters and/or brothers. The respondents' family size ranges from 2 to 6 (mean=4.35, SD=1.45). It should be noted that two thirds of the respondents (62, 66%) own their own houses.

Our respondents have been in the United States on the average for 8.1 years (SD=3.63). They have been in the self-employed small business on the average for 5.4 years (SD=2.97) in the United States. These two figures show that it took on the average 2.7 years for the respondents to start their own small business in the United States.

Over half of the respondents (52, 55.4%) report to have completed their college education prior to their emigration from Korea. In addition, five respondents have completed college education in the United States. This confirms that Korean small business owners are in general highly educated. Less than one third of the respondents (28, 29.8%) had some ex-

11

periences of managing their own business in Korea. A majority of them, however, had no such experiences prior to their emigration from Korea. They were employed in a variety of white collar occupations or had no occupational experience at all in Korea.

The majority of the respondents (57, 60.7%) report to have kin in the Chicago area. These kin are generally found to be parents, sisters and/or brothers of the respondents of their spouses. Three fourths of the respondents (68, 72.3%) have Korean friends in the Chicago area. Two thirds of the respondents (65, 69.1%) are affiliated with Korean churches, but only a small proportion of the respondents (26, 27.1%) participate in other Korean voluntary associations.

The above data show that most of the respondents maintain close ethnic social ties with their kin and friends. But beyond such primary group relationships, Korean churches are the only ethnic organization in which the respondents actively participate. The church is, however, a non-economic organization. This means that Korean immigrants maintain strong ethnic social ties with other Korean, but they have no powerful intermediate ethnic organizations which can effectively coordinate and regulate economic activities of Korean immigrants (Light, 1980).

In contrast, the respondents generally have no close social ties with whites or members of other ethnic groups. Only one fourth of the respondents (25, 26.6%) indicate to have white friends and even a smaller proportion of them (14, 14.9%) report to have friends who are members of other non-white ethnic groups. Only two respondents participate in American voluntary associations.

4. Data Analysis

We will first analyze the respondents' experience of business formation and then examine management in their first and current businesses respectively. Through this analysis, we will ascertain the work and family roles of the respondents and their spouses.

(1) Business Formation

Capital is undoubtedly one of the most crucial resources for business formation. How did the respondents obtain the initial capital, the capital invested in their first business in the United States? It appears that Korean small business owners obtain their initial capital in four ways: (1) the loan from American financial institutions, (2) money brought from home country, (3) family savings in the United States, and (4) the loan from their Korean friends or kin.

In order to test the respondents' methods of capital formation, the following question was given to the respondents: "Where was your own capital formed?" The respondents were then given two response categories: "mainly in Korea or mainly in the United States". Thirty percent of the respondents (28, 30.4%) indicated that their major capital (more than half of their own initial capital) was formed in Korea, while the majority (51, 55.4%) indicated that their major initial capital was formed in the United States. The remaining respondents (13, 14.2%) reported that their initial capital was formed in a similar proportion both in Korea and in the United States.

For the purpose of this research, those respondents whose major capital was formed in Korea will be referred to as "the Korean accumulators", while those whose major capital was formed in the United States, as "the American accumulators." Those whose major capital was formed in a similar proportion both in Korea and in the United States will be referred to as "the dual accumulators."

As the combined proportion of the American and dual accumulators (64, 69.6%) reveals, a great majority of the respondents formed a substantial proportion of their initial capital in the United States. How did the respondents form their own capital in the United States? The major source of their capital formation came from the saving of the earnings of the respondents and their family members. In addition to their own employment, both American and dual accumulators show that most of their spouses (45, 70.3%) were employed prior to the opening of the respondents' own business. Interestingly, a high proportion of the Korean accumulators (20, 74.1%) and their spouses (18) are also found to have been employed prior to the business entry of the respondents. All of the

14

employed spouses except four are found to be wives of the respondents.

The majority of the above employed male respondents (40, 56.6%) were blue-collar or service workers-assemblers, machinists, janitors, doormen, waiters, drivers, repairmen and so on. Other employed male respondents were either employees of Korean stores (11, 15.4%) or other types of white-collar workers (20, 28.1%). Most of the employed wives were either nurses (20, 37.7%) or blue-collar or service workers (21, 39.6%)—assemblers, janitresses, cooks, waitresses, and so on. The remaining employed wives (12, 22.7%) were white-collar employees such as technicians, receptionists, bank clerks, artists or employees of Korean stores. This employment experience reveals the kinds of jobs available to the respondents and their employed spouses in the American labor market prior to the opening of the respondents' own businesses.

Half of the respondents (43, 49%) show that their own initial capital was not enough to start out their first business and thus they borrowed additional capital from others. Most of these respondents did so from their own ethnic sources: their Korean friends (18), kin (17), banks (8) or other types of Koreans (3).

In addition to capital formation, business entry requires a variety of business preparation activities such as learning of the information of market opportunities, selection of the type of business invested, decision on the store location, legal registration of a new business, purchase of goods or services from suppliers, store layout, and learning of management practices including customer service. Those who start out their first business would naturally have no experience of business preparation, and therefore, need a great deal of help from others in coping with a number of formidable tasks of business preparation. How, then, did the respondents as newly arrived immigrants cope with such problems, especially when they opened their first business in the minority markets? Since the wives of the respondents were as inexperienced as the respondents for the above preparation activities, the wives could not help the respondents in such preparation activities. Under this condition, most of the help for these activities are found to come from the respondents' Korean friends or kin.

(2) First Business

The amount of the respondents' investment in their first business is found to have been very small. One third of the respondents (33, 35.7%) invested less than $10,000 in their first business. As a whole, three fourths of the respondents (71, 77%) invested less than $30,000 in their first business. The respondents invested their initial capital into the following four types of business: (1) clothing stores (18, 19.1%), (2) variety shops (20, 21.3%), (3) wig shops (19, 20.2%), and (4) other types of business (37, 30.4%).

With the limited amount of capital invested, their businesses generally required a considerable amount of labor. Thus, management of available labor resources becomes a critical issue for the survival and expansion of the immigrant businesses. Under this condition, a crucial question is: "Who provided labor for the operation of the respondent's first business?" We will examine this question in terms of the labor of the respondents, their spouses and employees.

As owner-operators, the respondents worked on the average for 58.1 hours (SD=13.9) a week in their first business. In addition, the majority of the spouses of the married respondents (47, 55.3%) worked on the average for 56.6 hours (SD=16) a week. This observation shows that the majority of the spouses participated in the operation of their family business generally as full-time workers. All of these spouses but two were wives of the respondents. In contrast, other family members did not work for the first business of the respondents. Only four respondents indicate that their children occasionally worked for their business and one respondent indicates that his nephew worked part-time. Half of the respondents obtained additional labor from their employment of workers. The majority of these respondents hired either one worker (25, 55.6%) or two workers (14, 31.3%). Only a few of the respondents hired more than two workers (6, 13.3%).

(3) Current Business

Most of the respondents (81, 86.1%) are retailers. Nine respondents operate service businesses such as Tae-Kwon Do Shop (1), snack shops (4) or laundry shops (4). Four respondents run wholesale busi-

17

nesses or the businesses which combine wholesale and retail businesses. The current businesses of the respondents can be classified into the following four types: (1) clothing shops (30, 31.9%), (2) variety shops (32, 34%), (3) shoe stores (12, 12.8%), and (4) other types of business (20, 21.3%).

As compared with the respondents' first business, the amount of investment in their current business has been considerably increased. One fifth of the respondents (21, 23.1%) have invested more than $100,000 in their current business and another one fifth (20, 21.9%) of them have invested $50,000 or more, but less than $100,000.

The majority of the respondents (56, 59.6%) open their stores for seven days a week, and one third of them (34, 36.2%) open their stores for six days a week, usually closing on Sundays. Four respondents (4.2%) indicate that they occasionally close their stores on Sundays and/or some other week days. Half of the spouses (49, 57.6%) are found to work at the stores of the respondents. Almost all of the spouses (47) are found to be the wives. The majority of these working wives also worked for the first business (34, 72.3%). Only one tenth of the respondents (10, 10.6%) indicate that their children or kin currently work at their stores.

The respondents who open their stores for seven days a week show that they work on the average 58.1 hours (SD=14.1) a week and their working spouses, 57.3 hours (SD=17.2). When the respondents open their stores for six days a week, they work on the average 53.8 hours (SD=12.1) a week, while their employed spouses work on the average 52.6 hours (SD=19.7). This observation shows that there is little difference in the average hours of work between the respondents and their working spouses, whether they work for seven days or six days a week. As a whole, the respondents work on the average for 56.5 hours (SD=13.3) and the employed spouses, for 54.2 hours (SD=18.5). These figures show that their current work hours are very similar to the work hours spent for their first business.

In contrast to the employment record for their first business, however, most of the respondents (69, 73.4%) hire workers for their current business. One fifth of the respondents (21, 22.3%) hire one employee and another one fifth (17, 18.1%) have two employees. One tenth of the respondents (13, 13.8%) hire three employees, while one fifth of the respondents (18, 19.2%) have 4 or more employees.

(4) Household Tasks

How does the business involvement of the wives affect the family roles of the wives and their husbands? In this research, we will measure only one aspect of the family role by focusing on the division of household tasks among family members.

Division of household tasks was examined by the following two questions: (1) Among your family members (e.g., wife, husband, and other members), how do you divide household tasks? (2) In your opinion, how should the household tasks be divided in principle? For the response, the following six items of household tasks were given: grocery shopping,

Table 1. Performance Patterns of Respondents' Families by Three Task Items (Grocery Shopping, House-Cleaning and Laundry)

	Grocery Shopping				House-Cleaning				Laundry			
	Behavior		Expectation		Behavior		Expectation		Behavior		Expectation	
	WN	WE	WN	WE	WN	WE	WN	WE	WN	WE	WN	WE
WP N	22	29	20	20	22	23	18	13	24	24	22	16
%	68.8	63.1	62.5	43.4	68.8	50.0	56.2	28.2	75.0	52.2	68.8	34.8
ES N	1	4	7	13	0	1	7	13	0	1	4	10
%	3.1	8.7	21.9	28.3	0	2.2	21.9	28.2	0	2.2	12.5	21.7
HP N	4	2	3	1	1	2	1	0	0	2	0	0
%	12.5	4.3	9.4	2.2	3.1	4.3	3.1	0	0	4.3	0	0
OT N	5	11	2	12	9	20	6	20	8	19	6	20
%	15.6	23.9	6.2	26.1	28.1	43.5	18.8	43.5	25.0	41.3	18.7	43.5
Total N	32	46	32	46	32	46	32	46	32	46	32	46
%	100.0	100.0	100.0	100.0	100.0	100.0	100.0	100.0	100.0	100.0	100.0	100.0

WN: Wife is not employed; WE: Wife is employed; WP: Wife performs predominantly; ES: Wife and husband share equally; HP: Husband performs predominantly; OT: Other members are involved.

Table 2. Performance Patterns of Respondents' Families by Three Task Items (Dishwashing, Garbage Disposal and Budget Management)

		Dishwashing				Garbage Disposal				Budget Management			
		Behavior		Expectation		Behavior		Expectation		Behavior		Expectation	
		WN	WE	WN	WE	WN	WE	WN	WE	WN	WE	WN	WE
WP	N	23	24	21	20	12	16	4	3	8	13	7	10
	%	71.9	52.2	65.6	43.5	37.5	34.8	12.5	6.5	25.0	28.2	21.9	21.7
ES	N	0	0	4	4	0	1	10	8	0	1	7	19
	%	0	0	12.5	8.7	0	2.2	31.3	17.4	0	2.2	21.9	41.3
HP	N	0	2	0	1	11	11	4	20	21	27	16	10
	%	0	4.3	0	2.1	34.4	23.9	12.5	43.5	65.6	58.7	50.0	21.8
OT	N	9	20	7	21	9	18	14	15	3	5	2	7
	%	28.1	43.5	21.9	45.7	28.1	39.1	43.7	32.6	9.4	10.9	6.2	15.2
Total	N	32	46	32	46	32	46	32	46	32	46	32	46
	%	100.0	100.0	100.0	100.0	100.0	100.0	100.0	100.0	100.0	100.0	100.0	100.0

WN: Wife is not employed; WE: Wife is employed; WP: Wife performs predominantly;
ES: Wife and husband share equally; HP: Husband performs predominantly;
OT: Other members are involved.

21

housekeeping, laundry, dishwashing, disposal of garbage, and management of family budget.

The respondents were then asked to rank their family members in terms of their relative performance of each of the above item.

Of the above two questions, the first deals with role behavior of family members—their performance of household tasks by virtue of their position in their family. The second deals with role expectation—their normative standard concerning division of household tasks in their family.

Analysis of the household tasks is based on only the married male respondents who answered the question of household tasks (76). Their responses to the task items are classified into the following four categories: (1) wife performs predominantly, (2) husband and wife perform equally, (3) husband performs predominantly, and (4) others are involved. The first category is a combination of two performance types, "wife performs alone," and "wife performs more than husband." The third category is a combination of two other performance types, "husband performs alone," and "husband performs more than wife." The last category includes all of the cases in which children or other kin (mother, sister, etc.) perform household tasks alone or with the wife and/or husband.

Data from the respondents will be analyzed separately by their wives' employment in the family business: "wife is employed" and "wife is not employed." In two task items, management of the family budget and disposal of garbage, husbands are expected to perform predominantly or to perform equally with their wives. Regardless of the business involvement of their wives, the majority of the husbands actually perform another tasks, disposal of garbage predominantly (see Tables 1 and 2).

In the remaining four task items, the husbands are seldom expected to perform predominantly, whether their wives are employed or not. Under this condition, the husbands are found to be virtually not involved in the actual performance of the four task items regardless of the business involvement of their wives (see Tables 1 and 2). In correspondence to the non-involvement of their husbands, the majority of the working wives are found to perform the four task items predominantly. This means that in addition to their full-time business involvement, most of the working wives perform the four items predominantly when they come home from work.

At the same time, we observe some effects of the work role of the wives on their family role. Relatively a smaller proportion of the working wives are expected to perform the four task items predominantly than the non-working wives. Under this condition, relatively a smaller proportion of the former actually perform the four items predominantly than the latter. In correspondence to this change, others (children or kin) in the families of the working wives are proportionally more expected to perform household tasks than the others in the families of the non-working wives. As a result, proportionally more children and kin in the families of the former are involved in the actual performance of the four task items than the ones in the families of the latter. This shows that some of the working wives shift in varying degrees their burden of household tasks to their children or kin (see Tables 1 and 2).

In sum, regardless of the business involvement of their wives, husbands in the Korean entrepreneurial families are not found to perform the four task items which have been traditionally regarded as the tasks of the wives. Nor are the husbands expected to perform these tasks, even when their wives work at their current stores as full-time workers. Under this condition, the majority of the working wives perform household tasks predominantly in addition to their full-time business involvement. Some of the working wives, however, shift some burden of performing the four household tasks to other members in their household but not to their husbands.

5. Discussion and Conclusions

This research has examined the work-family role experiences of Korean immigrants who are currently engaged in small business in the Chicago south side, the area of a heavy black concentration. Most of the respondents are found to be male, married and in economically active ages. They generally came to the United State with a high pre-immigration socioeconomic status, but with little small business experiences in Korea. Their current engagement in self employed small businesses appears to be a result of their socioeconomic adaptation to the

24

limited occupational opportunity available to them in the U.S. The limited occupational opportunity was evidenced by the nature of the jobs they held prior to their business entry. In this sense, the immigrants' current business operation may be considered as an emergent phenomenon which grew out of the opportunity structure open to the Korean immigrants in the United States and the immigrants' utilization of their own ethnic resources in response to such opportunity structure. In an effort to utilize ethnic resources, most of the wives of the Korean entrepreneurs have been involved in the various stages of business activities in spite of the traditional Korean marital roles which confine the wives to the home maker's role.

A notable feature of the respondents' business experiences is that they entered the self-employed small business on the average within three years of residence in the United States. Given the difficulties of the immigrants' adjustment, such as language problems, cultural barriers, and unfamiliarity with the American social system in general, one may wonder how the respondents managed to enter the field of small business so soon and also have managed to expand their businesses.

We have observed that the respondents formed their initial capital from three sources: (1) money brought from home country, (2) family savings in the United States, and (3) loan mainly from their Korean friends and kin. Of these three, the majority (nearly 70%) of our respondents relied heavily on the second source (family savings in the United States).

For this type of capital formation, most of the wives of the respondents had to be employed during the peirod of business preparation.

As an exploratory study, this research cannot determine the degree to which the employed wives have contributed to the formation of such initial capital. However, the nature of the jobs that their husbands held prior to the business entry shows that the husbands were generally employed for low-paying manual, service or white-collar jobs. This employment situation of the husbands suggests that their families probably needed employment of the wives for family support and/or saving of some family earnings during the period of capital formation.

When the respondents started out their first business, nearly half of their wives participated in the business operation generally as full-time workers. A similar proportion of the wives are found to work for the daily operation of the current business as full-time workers. These findings reveal that the extent of the wives' business involvement has not decreased in spite of the fact that the respondents have managed their own business on the average for more than five years and they expand their business scale considerably. Such business involvement of the wives may have contributed to the survival and expansion of their family business in two ways. First, as already mentioned, their business involvement as unpaid family workers would have definitely reduced the cost of labor in the labor-intensive business, and hence, enhanced the competitive advantage of their business. Second, self-employed small business owners in general are isolated from the mainstream in the U.S. economy and deprived of critical business-related information. Usually, however, they alone have to assume the major responsibility for all phases of their business activities, even the areas in which the owners lack any competence (Park and Chapin-Park, 1978). Under such deprived conditions, the business involvement of Korean immigrant wives would mean that they as trusted business collaborators assist the decision-making of their entrepreneurial husbands by offering numerous types of managerial advice. In sum the working wives play indispensable roles for the operation of the immigrant business by providing their own labor and managerial support.

Has this business involvement of the wives of the Korean entrepreneurs led to any modification of their traditional family roles? The data collected from the married male respondents fail to show any evidence that the business involvement of the wives increases the family role of the husbands as measured by their relative performance of household tasks. Under this condition, the majority of the working wives perform most of the household tasks in addition to their full-time work role. Some of the working wives, however, manage to share some burden of performing household tasks with their children or kin.

The data thus show that the wives of the Korean entrepreneurs generally carry a heavy burden of double roles, the work and family roles. The experience of this double burden is certainly not unique to the Korean working wives. It has repeatedly been observed that American working wives also suffer from the double burden (Araji, 1977; Berk, 1980; Berk and Berk, 1979; Blood and Wolfe, 1960; Pleck, 1977; Robinson, 1977; Stafford, Backman and Dibona, 1977; Vanke, 1980). In this context, an interesting fact is observed. Employment of American wives seem also to have a limited effect on the increase in their husbands' time for household tasks; however, the American working wives generally manage to reduce their own time for household tasks. Because of this reduced time of employed wives, American husbands' *relative* performance is generally found to increase in comparison with that of the wives, even though the actual amount of the husbands' time spent for household tasks may not necessarily much increase (Pleck, 1977). Surprisingly, even measured by such a relative performance, however, the Korean husbands are not found to increase their *relative* performance of the household tasks. Nor are the Korean husbands expected to perform more, even when their wives are employed. Such a uniform non-involvement of Korean immigrant husbands observed in both role behaviors and expectations suggests that the experience of the double burden of the Korean working wives is quite different from that of the American working wives.

The working wives' experience of the double burden together with the non-involvement of their husbands would mean that Korean working wives experience relatively more severe strain from the double burden than the American (especially white) wives. Such strain of the Korean wives may be further aggravated in general for two additional reasons. First, the immigrant wives are found to work for unusually long hours. Some of them also work for seven days a week. This suggests that the Korean working wives work more than the American working wives in terms of the time spent. This would in turn mean that the immigrant wives are more physically and psychologically exhausted, and thus, experience more difficulty in fulfilling expectations of different roles than their American counterparts. Second, as newcomers, Korean immigrant wives have been generally employed out of necessity without any adequate anticipatory socialization in the United States. Thus, it is likely that they experience more stress at their workplace than the native-born American working wives.

Korean husbands' non-involvement in the household tasks may be partly attributed to their past socialization of Korean traditional marital roles. Moreover, it appears that their current labor market conditions reinforce their orientation toward the traditional marital roles. As self-employed entrepreneurs, the Korean husbands must assume the major role for successful management of their business, and this requires them to engage in a variety of activities that include obtaining credits from various sources, keeping a good relationship with their suppliers, hiring and supervising their employees, customer services, store layout, and keeping vigilance for the business security. Aldous (1969) states that such occupational activities generally discourage the husbands to share the burden of performing household tasks. In addition, their long work hours would exhaust them physically and psychologically. Such work conditions hardly give them any stimulus to revise their orientation toward the traditional marital role, and to involve actively in the performance of household tasks. Under these work conditions, it is likely that even non-working wives would feel severely deprived of companionship and other marital support from their husbands.

Oakley (1974) stresses the subordinating and trivializing effects of the housewife's role in the modern society. As a solution to such problems, it has been generally suggested that the wife seeks out her own career outside home. Through immigration, the wives of Korean entrepreneurs have had a rare chance for working outside their home. Such an employment could give the Korean women a new opportunity to develop their own occupational career. But the nature of their current employment and accompaning problems do not seem to give them any meaningful opportunity to develop a new careerism. Rather, they seem to regard employment as a necessity in their struggle to establish a minimum economic security for their families in the United States. As long as this condition persists, they may have to continuously be involved in the daily operation of their family business. Under this condition, the Korean wives' work orientation may fit what Ewer,

Crimmis and Oliver observe from some American working wives: "Even in working, the wives appear to be reacting more to traditional (i.e., family supporting) wife/mother role expectations than in terms of the self-fulfillment career model idealized by the feminist movement" (1979: 737).

To conclude, our exploratory study of the immigrant working wives reveal many significant sources of the immigrants' adaptation problems in the United States. The double burden that Korean immigrant wives carry is certainly a joint product of structural, situational, and cultural factors derived from immigration—the American socioeconomic structure (the disadvantaged labor market for immigrants, business opportunity in the labor-intensive industries), the immigrants' adaptive capacities and limitations (ethnic resources utilization, language and other problems), and persisting traditional values and norms in the new country (the wife's home maker's role regardless of her employment). For the future research, therefore, we suggest to search out the practical and theoretical implications of the double burden carried by Korean entrepreneurs' wives and related adaptation problems in multiple perspectives.

References

Aldous, Joan
1969 "Occupational characteristics and males' role performance in the family," Journal of Marriage and the Family 31:707-712.

Araji, Sharon K.
1977 "Husbands' and wives' attitude-behavior congruence on Family roles," Journal of Marriage and Family 39:309-320.

Bahr, S. J.
1974 "Effects on power and division of labor in the family," pp. 161-185 in L. W. Hoffman and F. I. Nye (eds.)., Working Mothers, San Francisco: Jossey-Bass.

Barheide, Catherine White and Esther Ngan-Ling Chow
1983 "The interdependence of family and work: some models and proposals," A paper presented at the annual meeting of The American Sociological Association, August 31 - September 4, Detroit, Michigan

Berk, Sarah F. (ed.)
1980 Women and Household Labor. Beverly Hills, Calif.: Sage Publication.

Berk, Richard and Sarah F. Berk
1979 Labor and Leisure at Home: Content and Organization of the Household Day. Beverly Hills, Calif.: Sage Publication.

Blood, Robert O. and Donald M. Wolfe
1960 Husbands and Wives. New York: The Free Press.

Bonacich, Edna
1972 "A theory of ethnic antagonism: the split labor market," American Sociological Review 37, pp. 583-559.
1973 "A theory of middleman minorities," American Sociological Review 38 (Oct.), pp. 583-594.

1978 "U.S. capitalism and Korean immigrant small business: a study in the relationship between class and ethnicity," a paper presented at the ninth World Congress of Sociology in Uppsala, Sweden.

Bonacich, Edna and Tae Whan Jung
1982 "A portrait of Korean small business in Los Angeles, 1977," pp. 75-98 in Eui-Young Yu, Earl H. Phillips (eds.), Koreans in Los Angeles: Prospects and Promises, Los Angeles, Calif.: Koryo Research Insitute, Center for Korean-American and Korean Studies, California State University, Los Angeles.

Bonacich, Edna, Ivan Light, and Charles Choy Wong
1980 "Korean immigrants: small business in Los

Angeles," pp. 167-184 in Roy Simon Bryce-Laporte (ed.), Sourcebook on the New Immigration. New Brunswick, New Jersey: Transaction Books.

Bonacich, Edna and John Modell
1980 The Economic Basis of Ethnic Solidarity.
Los Angeles: University of California Press.

Bowling, Michael
1977 "Sex role attitudes and division of household labor," A paper presented at the annual meeting of American Sociological Association, Chicago, September 5-9.

Bryce-Laporte, Roy Simon (ed.)
1980 Sourcebook on the New Immigration: Implications for the United States and International Community. New Brunswick, New Jersey: Transaction Books.

Burr, Wesley R.
1972 "Role transitions: a reformulation of theory," Journal of Marriage and the Family 34:407-416.

Chafe, William H.
1976 "Looking backward in order to look forward: women, work, and social values in America," pp. 6-30 in Juanita M. Kreps (ed.), Women and The American Economy: A Look to the 1980's. Englewood Cliffs, New Jersey: Prentice-Hall, Inc.

Choi, Jai-Seuk
 1977 "Family system," Korean Journal 17 (May):
4-14.

Doctors, Samuel I. and Anne Sigismund Huff (eds.)
 1973 Minority Enterprise and the President's
Council. Cambridge, Mass.: Ballinger Publishing Co.

Ewer, Phyllis A., Eileen Crimmis and Richard Oliver
 1979 "An analysis of the relationship between
husband's income, family size and wife's employment in the early stages of marriage," Journal of
Marriage and the Family 41:727-738.

Feinstein, Karen Wolk (ed.)
 1979 Working Women and Families. Beverly
Hills, Calif.: Sage Publication.

Ferber, Marianne A.
 1982 "Labor market participation of young married women: causes and effects," Journal of Marriage
and the Family 44:457-468.

Fleming, Sundar W.
 1979 "Buy minority' or the marketing concept? A
vital choice for minority business." Journal of Small
Business Management 17 (Oct.), pp. 18-21.

Freedmand, Jonathan L.
 1978 Happy People: What Happiness Is, Who
Has It and Why. New York: Harcourt, Brace and
Jovanovich.

Hayghe, Howard
1976 "Families and the rise of working wives: an overview," Monthly Labor Review 99 (Summer): 12-19.

Hurh, Won Moo and Kwang Chung Kim
1984 Korean Immigrants in America: A Structural Analysis of Ethnic Confinement and Adhesive Adaptation. Madison, New Jersey: Fairleigh Dickinson University Press.

Jin, Hyung-Ki
1978 A Survey on Economic and Managerial Status on Korean Businesses in the Los Angeles Area (Korean). Los Angeles, Calif.: Korean Chamber of Commerce of Southern California.

Kanter, Rosabeth Moss
1977 Work and Family in the United States: A Critical Review and Agenda for Research and Policy. New York: Russell Sage Foundation.

Kim, David S. and Charles Choy Wong
1977 "Business development in Koreatown, Los Angeles," pp.229-245 in Hyung-Chan Kim (ed.), The Korean Diaspora. Santa Barbara, Calif.: ABC-Clio, Inc.

Kim, Haeng-Ja
1978 "Dormant feminine power," Korea Journal 18 (Oct.): 11-14.

Kim, Hyon-Ja
1971 "The changing role of women in Korea,"
Korea Journal 11 (May): 21-24.

Kim, Hyung-Chan
1977 "Ethnic enterprises among Korean immigrants in America," pp. 85-107 in Hyung-Chan Kim (ed.), The Korea Diaspora. Santa Barbara, Calif.: ABC-Clio, Inc.

Kim, Ill Soo
1981 New Urban Immigrants: The Korean Community in New York. Princeton, New Jersey: Princeton University Press.

Ledvinka, James and William W. Pearson
1971 "On developing new minority businessmen," Journal of Small Business Management 9 (Jan.), pp. 26-30.

Lee, Hae-Young
1978 "Family," pp. 755-814 in Hae Young Lee and Tai Hwan Kwon (eds.), Hankul Sahae: Inku Wa Balchun (Korean Society: Population and Development). Seoul, Korea: Research Institute of Population and Development, Seoul National University.

Lee, Hyo-Chai
1973 "Changing Korean Family and the Old," Korea Journal 13 (June): 20-25.

Lee, Hyo-Chai and Cho Hyoung
1977 "Fertility and women's labor force participation in Korea," Korea Journal 17 (July): 12-34.

Light, Ivan
1972 Ethnic Enterprise in America. Berkeley, Calif.: University of California Press.

1980 "Asian enterprise in America: Chinese, Japanese and Korean in small business," pp. 35-57 in Scott Cummings (ed.), Self-Help in Urban America. Port Washington, New York: Kennikat Press.

1979 "Disadvantaged minorities in self-employment," International Journal of Comparative Sociology XX (1-2): 31-45.

Lovell-Troy, Lawrence A.
1980 "Clan structure and economic activity: the case of Greeks in small business enterprise," pp. 58-85 in Scott Cummings (ed.), Self-Help in Urban America: Patterns of Minority Business Enterprise, Port Washington, New York: Kennikat Press.

Mason, Karen O., John L. Czajka and Sarah Arber
1976 "Change in U.S. Women's sex-role attitudes, 1964-1974," American Sociological Review 41: 573-596.

MBDA Research Division (Minority Business Development Agency)
1982 Minority Business Enterprise Today: Prob-

lems and Their Causes.

Oakley, Ann
1974 Women's Work: The Housewife Past and
Present. New York: Pantheon Books.

Park, William R. and Sue Chapin Park
1978 How to Succeed in Your Own Business. New
York: John Wiley and Sons.

Pleck, Joseph H.
1977 "The work-family role system," Social Problems 2 (April): 417-427.

Robinson, John P.
1977 How Americans Use Their Time. New York:
Praeger.

Robinson, John P., Thomas Justin and Frank
Stafford
1976 American's Use of Time. Ann Arbor,
Michigan: Institute for Social Research, The University of Michigan.

Slocum, Walter L. and F. Ivan Nye
1976 "Provider and housekeeper roles," pp. 81-99
in F. Ivan Nye (ed.), Role Stucture and Analysis of
the Family. Beverly Hills, Calif.: Sage Publications.

Stafford, Rebecca, Elaine Backman and Pamela
Dibona
1977 "The division of labor among cohabiting and

married couples," Journal of Marriage and the Family 39:43-57.

The State of Small Buiness: A Report of the President
1982 Washington, D.C.: U.S. Government Printing Office.

Vanek, Joann
1980 "Household work, wage work, and sexual equality," pp. 275-291, in Sarah F. Berk (ed.), Women and Household Labor. Beverly Hills, Calif.: Sage Publication.

Waldinger, Roger D.
1982 "Immigrant enterprise and labor market structure," a paper presented at the 77th annual meeting of American Sociological Association, September 6-10, 1982, San Francisco, Calif.

1983 "Ethnic enterprise: a critique and reformulation," a paper presented at the 78th annual meeting of American Sociological Association, Aug. 31 Sept. 4, 1983, Detroit, Michigan.

Walker, Kathryn E.
1959 "Time spent in household work by homemakers," Family Economic Review 4:8-11.

Wilson, Kenneth L. and Alejandro Portes
1980 "Immigrant enclaves: an analysis of the labor market experiences of Cubans in Miami," American Journal of Sociology 86:295-319.

Wilson, Kenneth L. and W. Allen Martin
    1982 "Ethnic enclaves: a comparison of the Cuban
and black economies in Miami," American Journal of
Sociology 88:135-160.

Transcultural Marriage and Its Impact on Korean Immigration*

Daniel B. Lee

1. Introduction

The social phenomenon of transcultural marriage between Korean women and American military personnel must be examined from both historical and ontological perspectives since it bears significant consequences for Korean immigration in the United States and overseas. During the past three decades, nearly 80,000 Korean women emigrated to the U.S. as dependents of American servicemen.[1] In addition, the majority subsequently brought their Korean relatives to this "promised land" in order to fulfill the duties of filial piety and to cushion their cultural isolation. These women have smoothed and paved the rugged inroads for successive followers in transcultural marriage. They also have widened the highways of cultural transition for their fellow country people's immigration journey of adjustment and exploration of new possibilities in a new land. Quietly they have placed countless cornerstones on the spiritual foundations of ethnic churches.[2] They have built bridges of cross-cultural understanding between the East and the West. They have also contributed much patronage to Korean-American business. As an integral part of the Korean-American community, the role of transculturally married Korean women continues to have far-reaching consequences for the course of the unfolding history of migration. By virtue of their culture-transcending marriages, they have unique and intimate positions which connect a wide spectrum of socio-political decision making processes. Through parenting, their aspirations and dreams for transcultural harmony and success may well be fulfilled by their American offspring.

Until very recent years, there was a gross neglect and underestimation of the significance of the role that transcultural marriage has played in the course of Korean immigration, Korean-American relations, and transculturation of people across boundaries of nationality, creed, and ethnicity. In order to redress this neglect, the author conceptualizes transcultural marriage from an ontological perspective, and develops a balanced conceptual framework from which to examine both its pitfalls and promises. From the author's cumulative clinical experience, empirical research and participatory observation, several theoretical propositions are developed regarding the typology of transcultural marriage styles, characteristics of psychosocial strength and strain associated with transcultural marriage, and developmental phases of intercultural adjustment.[3]

While examining some more positive aspects of transcultural marriage, a number of unresolved issues are identified in the context of social

43

ministries. Social implications for "Minjung" theology are explicated for an indepth analysis of current experiences of in-group alienation and insensitivity, victimization and exploitation, and enforced marginality. Case examples will illustrate poignantly the various afflictions of those who experience difficulty in the transculturation process. The complexity of problems associated with culturally disoriented or deprived women of Korean ancestry demands a multidimensional approach to its attempted solution.[4] Therefore, the author offers some practical suggestions for developing a systematic and comprehensive service program model. An ontological viewpoint on the experience of transcultural marriage is advanced in concluding the presentation.

Concept of Transcultural Marriage

Transcultural marriage is an expanding phenomenon in our contemporary society as people are increasingly mobile across geographical, cultural, and state boundaries. In this context of transcultural interactions, which is historically accounted in many parts of the world, people of diverse cultural backgrounds come together in realization of a universal tendency to meet basic human needs through the foundational social institutions of marriage and family. Slowly, recognizing this trend as a profound and valuable development is growing as an alternative approach to traditionally proscriptive positions held by many societies, including Korea

44

and the United States.[5]

"Transcultural" as defined in the Webster Third New International Dictionary refers to "extending through all human cultures or types of human beings."[6] The marriages of people extending through various cultural characteristics such a race, nationality, religion, customs and language may be called "transcultural marriages" as broadly defined. Transcultural marriage is defined here as a marriage that is constituted by spouses of two divergent cultural backgrounds across national and racial and/or ethnic boundaries.

Here, the concept "transcultural" denotes the characteriztion of a global community that is becoming more and more a reality to all human races extending through cultural boundaries conditioned by geographic isolation, inborn traits of skin color, nationality, religion, language, and other socioeconomic forces. The development of a global community works toward the ultimate synthesis of humanity, as it embraces our understanding of dynamic elements underlying humanism that transcends various obstacles and barriers—both psychological and sociological in nature. Transcultural marriages require added dimensions such as intercultural competence and durable commitment to humanism if their full potentiality is to be realized. As developed in the above statement, if the only meaningful basis upon which one can compare social and cultural traits is in terms of the ethnic group, then transcultural marriage is more conceptually sound and ontological than other descriptive terminologies of intermarriage such as interracial, mixed, international, etc. that are defined rather restrictively.

In contrast to the majority of the studies on intermarriage in the U.S., which have been focused on the rates, patterns, theories, and consequences of such incidences in the context of prevailing American ethnocentricism with specific references to race and religion, the author expands the concept of transcultural marriages beyond the sociological concept of "ingroup vs. outgroup" boundaries as discussed by Merton.[7]

Social Context

Barron has suggested that institutional and normative restrictions of intermarriage have become ineffective since the 1960's in industrialized societies generally, and the United States in particular. The high American priority of personal choice in marriage overrides such restrictive controls.

Adams postulated the breakdown of psychological boundaries among people of different cultural backgrounds through intimate human interactions.[8]

Like many other war-torn countries, Korea has been struggling with her modernizaion for the postwar period of over 30 years. Unlike her neighboring country, Japan, Korea still is facing the threat of the communist invasion from North Korea with a heavy burden of a large defense budget and psychological insecurity. The security policy of the U.S. toward Korea discussed by Johnson and others

46

emphasizes the credibility of the commitment made to the Republic of Korea in the mutual defense treaty of October 1, 1953. Since the withdrawal of most U.S. military personnel from Indochina, South Korea is made tangible by an infantry division, four squadrons of fighter-bombers and tactical nuclear weapons.[9]

From what has been said, one cannot sufficiently infer the sociocultural aspects and real life situations linked with the presence of American servicemen in the Korean environments. Despite the strength of South Korea's economic growth and opposition to communism, rapid changes in migration patterns, values, and attitudes away from her traditional kinship oriented socialization have created a major challenge to societal adaptation. The contemporary increase of self-centered individualization has resulted in transitory social malaise, conflicting with the norms of traditional society. The prolonged presence of relatively rich American forces throughout the country attracts a large number of opportunity-seeking individuals. Among them are those "disposed" migrants whose socio-economic needs are often disregarded by the large society and exploited commercially by the mediator, purveyors of vice. Although more opportunities for education and employment have opened to women in the recent years of industrialization in Korea, its traditional patriarchal family system and the inferior social status of women that is structurally patterned in its cultural environment still limit upward mobility of women, those in particular with low socio-economic family backgrounds. As education and social membership lingkage reinforce the range of upward mobility in this highly competitive society, one who is destined to a severely limited opportunity for individual growth and social well-being often chooses culturally deviant ways to compensate for her disadvantage or to achieve certain goals—immediate relief from her destitution. Under these circumstances, transcultural interactions often are motivated between American servicemen who are culturally displaced and emotionally isolated and their Korean counterparts who wish to pursue opportunities for social mobility and economic advancement.

Kim describes the backgrounds of those unfortunate women in Korea as "the victims of the Korean War and rapid westernization in Korea," as he depicts their paradoxical dilemma. As he says, maid-service provided by a woman from a low income family can be tantamount to slavery, whereas a bar girl position has better financial incentive although it is degrading. Her alternatives are to be "a good girl with no hope" or "a bad girl with some hope." As T. Lee Hughes explained in the Korea Times newspaper, G.I. marriage is sometimes the result of contacts between poorly educated U.S. G.I.s and desperate Korean prostitutes—with unfortunate results. General Donald V. Bennett, then Commander-in-Chief of the U.N. in Korea, described the pathological growth of "G.I. Town" clip joints, prostitution, venereal disease and other vices which result from mutual exploitation by disadvantaged or emotionally deprived Americans and Koreans. He advocated improvement of community programs to counter this tendency. Unfortunately, the negative characterization of those who engage in trans-cultural marriages and G.I. town environments only reinforces the prejudicial stereotyping of subcultural characteristics that are often viewed as undesirable elements in our society. Even in the professional journals, the backgrounds of Korean wives of American servicemen are characterized by the un-favorable statement, "very few women met their husbands through legitimate work; most women met them while working as prostitutes."[10]

McCullagh provides comprehensive demographic data on U.S. servicemen who married Koreans while stationed in Korea. Unlike other studies cited, his in-vestigation is objective and reliable in validating his findings on the characteristics of these unions. In his study of 264 randomly selected transcultural mar-riage applicants filed in 1972, McCullagh concluded that the facts do not support the common assump-tions that most such marriages fail or that the ma-jority of girls married by soldiers are prostitutes.

Impact on Korean Immigration to the United States

The prolonged presence of some 40,000 U.S. military personnel in Korea since the end of Korean conflict in 1953 has had a direct impact on the suc-cessive increase of such marriages as shown in Table 1. The influx of recent Korean immigrants to the U.S., representing the second largest Asian immigrant group, is largely the result of such unions.

Table 1

TRENDS OF THE TRANSCULTURAL
MARRIAGES IN KOREA

1956 - 1979

Year	Number	Cumulative Total+
1956	140	140
1957	416	556
1958	480	1,036
1959	758	1,794
1960	805	2,599
1961	975	3,574
1962	1,435	5,009
1963	1,645	6,654
1964	1,625	8,279
1965	1,647	9,926
1966	1,686	11,612
1967	1,624	13,236
1968	2,310	15,546
1969	2,608	18,154
1970	3,808	21,962
1971	4,895	26,857
1972	4,483	31,340
1973	4,791	36,340
1974	4,220	40,351
1975	4,738	45,089
1976	5,665	50,754
1977	5,520	56,274
1978	5,026	61,300
1979	4,043	65,343

A report by the Korean Development Institute on Korean emigrants shows that nearly half the emigrants during 1962 and 1963 were married to American servicemen. As Table 2 indicates, comparing transculturally married Korean immigrants with other types, nearly all are women who have emigrated as spouses or fiances. The majority were comparatively disadvantaged by less than six years of education, unemployment, and the necessity of renting a home. Finally, it is important to note the magnitude of Korean-American military transcultural marriages. The author estimates that more than 60,000 of these have occurred since 1950; the majority of families continuing to reside near major U.S. military installations.[12]

Table 2 DEMOGRAPHIC CHARACTERISTICS OF TRANSCULTURALLY MARRIED KOREAN IMMIGRANTS BY COMPARING GROUPS ACROSS SEX, EDUCATION AND MARITAL STATUS*

	Transcultural Marriage Group (N=2,126)	Other Types of Immigrants — Family Immigrants (N=3,768)	Other Types of Immigrants — Employment Immigrants (N=1,369)
Sex			
Male	1.9%	49.0%	54.9%
Female	98.1%	51.0%	36.7%
Education			
No Formal Schooling	26.4%	8.5%	1.4%
Less than 6th Grade	1.8%	1.5%	0.1%
6th Grade Completed	35.0%	15.7%	4.5%
9th Grade Completed	14.1%	12.3%	10.9%
High School Completed	18.6%	35.6%	29.4%
College Graduate	4.0%	26.3%	53.7%
Other Non-Classified	0.1%	–	0.1%
Marital Status			
Married	66.8%	65.4%	69.4%
Single	–	23.2%	28.7%
Engaged	31.9%	1.4%	–
Remarried	1.3%	1.3%	0.3%
Separated	–	0.1%	–
Divorced	–	0.3%	0.1%
Widowed	–	8.2%	1.2%
Other Non-Classified	–	0.2%	0.3%
Total Percentage	100 %	100 %	100 %

*Reconstructed from the Korean Development Institute Series Report on *the Study of Korean Overseas Immigrants*, 1979, pp. 114-116.

52

A Case Illustration

Simsoon, a 38-year old Korean woman, accompanied her Army staff sergeant husband to Florida. During more than two years' residence there, she experienced increasing difficulty making friends with either her own or her husband's ethnic backgrounds. This contributed to an identity crisis including confusion, cognitive dissonance, and hypersensitivity. She began to internalize a sense of inadequacy, social deprivation, and loss of self-control. In this condition of vulnerability, she attempted suicide when she heard the news of her blind father's serious health condition back home. Upon recovery from the unsuccessful suicide attempt, she revealed her deepseated feeling of guilt for leaving her impoverished family behind in order to pursue her own happiness. Her unfulfilled obligation of filial piety to her parents stimulated this dramatic action. Her several previous attempts to pressure her husband to obtain a compassionate reassignment to Korea had failed. Since she could not return to Korea in her body, she tried at least to free her soul to return.[13]

Various social networks are formed during this initial adjustment phase to ward off social and psychological alienation. More than half of Korean spouses, for instance, have brought out their relatives to the United States as a way to incorporate their natal family support system within their new environment. Contrary to initial expectations, interaction with relatives often introduces another wide spectrum of psychosocial stresses including value conflicts, competition, jealousy, and financial burden. The relatives may even be reluctant to disclose their association with their Korean-American kin because of bias against transcultural marriage. This may increase Korean spouse's sense of alienation from her own ethnic group as well as her husband's. Therefore, the outcome of restructuring an extended family network involves mixed blessings and woes. This pattern of bias and stigmatization against military transcultural marriage is often repeated in the general Korean community, thereby increasing experiences of strain within the intraethnic social network. Such in-group prejudice operates as a stressor for many Asian spouses, not only Koreans. As a result of accumulated frustration in attempts to establish an intraethnic support system, Asian spouses often form their own transculturally married supported subgroup.[14]

Sil Dong Kim examined 94 interracially married Korean women immigrants in the Seattle-Tacoma area. He concluded that their various social networks are directed to the immunization of the members against the feelings, negative values and attitudes arising from successive failures during the period of their struggles for survival in America. Traditional cultural values such as euri (loyalty), chae-noem (resignation), and familialism have supported these protective community ties. He indicates that these women are apt to accept their own present sacrifice for the future benefit of their husbands and children.[15]

Impact of Transcultural Marriage on Korean Immigration

Obviously, transcultural marriage between Korean women and American military personnel has greatly accelerated and increased the amount of Korean immigration to the United States. In addition to this numerical impact, there are very profound results upon Korean ethnic communities as well as Korean-American interrelations.

First of all, Korean spouses of American husbands exist in a constant bicultural family context which necessarily stimulates adjustment strategies directed toward cross-cultural integration. These Korean women can therefore be regarded as indigenous "experts" on Korean-American relations. Together with their American spouses and Amerasian children, they develop countless informal ways of bringing together East and West, thereby fostering the transformation of Korean monoculturalism into new forms of cultural pluralism. They also act as mediators of Korean culture to American society as whole, not only by association with in-laws, but also be spreading cultural information through ethnic community celebrations open to the public, exhibiting traditional artworks at community functions, and raising awareness of Koreans in their children's school systems. Indeed, the children of transcultural marriages become the living embodiments of cultural synthesis. In addition, Korean wives have often given social financial support to visiting Korean students.[16]

Secondly, the strong Korean values of filial piety and family support have prompted Korean wives to continue strong relations with natal families in Korea, thus forging an international link. Korean wives may even send monetary support to their natal families to help pay debts and siblings' tuition fees. In order to create an ethnic family self-support system and also to help relatives to advance their fortunes, Korean wives often sponsor the emigration of their natal family members. They therefore smooth the process of immigration by providing host country-based support as well as experience tested models of successful adjustment.

Thirdly, Korean wives have been important in developing Korean community associations, international wives associations, and other ethnic support groups. Especially in the proximity of major military installations, Korean wives of servicemen and their relatives typically compose 60 or more of the Korean-American local population. This fact has major significance for the growth of Korean ethnic churches. Korean wives are often active church members and organizers. They provide financial support for the church members and its minister. Importantly, they also challenge the ethnic churches to meet their unique bicultural and bilingual needs—both on practical and spiritual levels. Thus, they become catalysts for the transcultural adaptation of Korean christian ministry. Another consequence of their prominence in Korean ethnic communities is their operation or patronage of Korean-American business.

Fourth, the transcultural family is a national interface between Korean and American communities which engenders processes of assimilation and transculturation. Korean-American families become prototypes for future generations' efforts toward cross-cultural adjustment. In particular, successful Korean-American marriages serve as encouragement for second and third generation Korean-Americans (mostly women) to carry members of non-Korean-American ethnic groups. Future generations can learn many valuable lessons for transcultural accommodation from the successes and failures of the first generation transcultural marriages.[17]

Korean-American transcultural families are truly the pioneers of the transculturation process; that is, the actualization of the global family of love which includes all people regardless of race, culture, or nationality. No longer are people limited to narrow monocultural perspectives, values, and behaviors. In the contemporary world, profoundly influenced by transcultural families, it is now possible to develop panhuman, universal perspectives, values, and behaviors which can make possible harmony among all people.

Conclusion: Implications for Social Ministries

In concluding this article, the author recommends that a system of collective efforts be developed in the form of social ministries to reach out to many culturally deprived individuals and to appreciate contributions made by many successful Korean women of transcultural marriage. In doing so, three major objectives of such ministry are thought out as follows:

The first objective shall be to raise social consciousness and self awareness among the transculturally married individuals and families toward clarification and better understanding of the myths and realities of intermarriage and its associated consequences and challenges in the context of intra and interethnic relations.[18]

The second objective shall be to systematically assess concerns and needs of the target population and its associated public sectors with regards to the nature of barriers and handicaps in achieving desirable living and success of transcultural adjustment and integration.

The third and final objective shall be to organize ethnic and church community resources, public and voluntary or private, for the establishment of area community service networks geared to holistic program development and sensitivity to the needs of the target population.[20]

The unresolved problem here is that due to a lack of sophisticated program design, systematic program implementation, and poor logistical support, only a small proportion of the Korean spouses seem to have participated in the organized acculturation programs. A permanent transcultural orientation program needs to be jointly developed at the U.S. military installations throughout Korea and the U.S. by appropriate agencies of both Korean and

American governments. The major military installations in cooperation with Korean churches, local social agencies and educational systems need to develop an ongoing transcultural orientation program for incoming Korean-American transcultural families. Periodical transcultural training programs need to be developed locally and nationwide for the helping professionals, Korean ministers, interested military authorities, and volunteers. The programs should include not only acculturation content but also implications of mental health, intergroup relationships and marital adjustment. American husbands and their relatives also need to engage in all phases of their Korean spouses' adjustment to American cultural systems, as noted in the successful couples of transcultural marriage.

NOTES

[1]See the Table 1 on page 7 below. Over 90% of all Koreans who were internationally married have emigrated to the U.S. Of these, the great majority are married to American Servicemen.

[2]Nearly all of Korean local churches are currently membered by the transculturally married women and their relatives in the communities where the U.S. military installations are located. They play an important role in establishing, maintaining and developing local ethnic minority churches.

[3]Daniel B. Lee, "Asian-Born Spouses: Stresses and Coping Patterns," *Military Family 2*, (March-April, 1982): 3-5. The author has delineated four types of transcultural marriage based on motivational dynamics. These are survival, exchange, challenge and altruistic types.

[4]Bok-Lim C. Kim has written several articles on "Asian Women in Shadow." Idem, "Casework with Japanese and Korean Wives of Americans," *Social Casework*, 53 (1972): 273-279; Idem, "Asian Wives of U.S. Servicemen: Women in Shadows," *Amerasia Journal*, 4 (1974): 91-115; B-L C. Kim, A.I. Okamura, N. Ozawa, and V. Forrest, *Women in Shadows* (La Jolla, Ca.: The National Committee Concerned with Asian Wives of U.S. Servicemen, 1981).

[5]Proscriptive biases were reflected in the works of the following social scientist, on the subject of intermarriage in 1960's and 1970's; M.S. Barron, "Intergroup Aspects of Choosing a Mate," In Idem, ed., *The Blending American: Patterns of Intermarriage* (Chicage: Quadrangle Books, 1972); G. DeVos, "Ethnic Pluralism: Conflict and Accommodation," *In Ethnic Identity: Cultural Continuities and Change* (Palo Alto, CA: Mayfield, 1975); (G. DeVos and L. Romanucch-Ross, eds); A. Gordon, *Intermarriage: Interfaith, Interracial, Interethnic,* (Boston: Beacon Press, 1984); and A. Kiev, "Psychiatric Implications of Interracial Marriage," In I. Stuart & L. Abt., eds., *Interracial Marriage: Expectation and Realities* (New York: Grossman Publishers, 1973).

[6]*Webster Third International Dictionary of the English Language* (Springfield, Mass.: GEC Merriam, 1964), p. 2429.

[7]Milton Barron, "The Church, the State and Intermarriage," In Idem, ed., *Blending American.*

[8]Raymond Adams, *International Marriage in Hawaii: A Study of the Mutually Conditioned Process of Acculturation and Amalgamation* (New York: MacMillan, 1937).

[9]Samuel Johnson, *The Military Equation in Northeast Asia* (Washington, D.C.: The Brookings Institute, 1979).

[10]Sil Dong Kim, *Interracially Married Korean Immigrants: A Study in Marginality* (Ph. D. Dissertation, University of Washington, 1979), pp. 1-39; Korea Times (Friday, February, 1967), p. 3; *Pacific Stars and Stripes* (November 2, 1972), p. 7; Kim Casework, p. 277.

[11]Chaplain McCullagh at the Headquarters, Eighth U.S. Army studied 264 randomly selected transcultural marriage applicants in 1972 and his demographic findings indicated that 59 of Korean girls did not have employment; 15 had verified legitimate occupation; 14 worked as clerks at shops and stores; 10 worked in clubs and tearooms. His detailed report in the minutes of the Human Self Development and Planning Unit, the Office of Eighth U.S. Army Chaplains (25 September 1973) under the title: "A Study of the International Marriage between American Servicemen and Koreans." Sawon Hong did a similar socio-demographic survey of 351 Korean women who were either engaged or married to American servicemen and who had applied for permission to emigrate in 1978. Her data revealed that 37.5 percent had had no job experience before or after marriage. The most common types of work for these women (53.8 percent) were in the services sector. See S. Hong, "Another Look at Marriages between Korean Women and American Servicemen," *Korea Journal,* 22 (May, 1982): pp. 21-30.

[12]Korean Development Institute, *A Study of Korean Overseas Immigrants* (Korean language,

Research Report, Seoul: KDI, 1979) pp. 114-116. See also Daniel Lee, *Military Transcultural Marriage: A Study of Marital Adjustment between American Husbands and Korean-born Spouses* (Ph.D. Dissertation, University of Utah, 1980), pp. 15-17, and 48-55.

[13]This case was actually seen at the U.S. Army Hospital Mental Health Clinic, Yong San, Korea by the author while assigned there as the Chief Social Work Officer during 1973-75.

[14]The author found that one of the social characteristics associated with these marriages is sociocultural isolation: The more strain the marriage experiences, the more isolation from which they seem to suffer. Lee, Asian-Born Spouses, p. 4.

[15]Kim, *Interracially Married Korean Immigrants*, pp. 160-163.

[16]Daniel Lee, "Asian-Born Spouses and American In-laws: Challenge for Transcultural Community Building," *Military Family* (May-June 1984): 3-6. Most Korean students who came to the United States for study abroad during 1960's and 1970's had witnessed those warm hospitality and country-fellowship rendered by the transculturally married Korean sisters.

[17]Similar to the assimilation of the second and third generations of other Asian immigrants, it is

highly probable that the rate of intermarriage among the succeeding generations of Korean immigrants will increase to fifty percent within the next few decades.

[18]Man Keung Ho, *Building Successful Intermarriage* (St. Meinrad, Ind.: Abbey Press, 1984).

[19]Slowly but more recently the U.S. Military System as an institution began to formulate and implement its worldwide family policy inclusive of the so-called, "Bi-cultural Families." Such policy demands a comprehensive needs assessments of Korean American families within the military system. See the *Army Family Action Plan* (Community and Family Policy Division, Human Resources Development Directorate Office of the Deputy Chief for Personnel, 1984). p. 26.

[20]More immediate and proactive attentions should be given by major christian denominations to the needs for developing effective social ministries to the Korean-American transcultural families both in America and abroad.

The Social Reality of the Korean-American Women: Toward Crashing with the Confucian Ideology

Minza Kim Boo

1. Introduction

The cultural heritage and traditional values of Korea have been derived and evolved from various sources such as Shamanism, Buddhism, Taoism, Confucianism, Kyung Chun Sa Sang, Sill Hak Sa Sang, etc. Confucianism has, however, been the mainstream of Korean culture and tradition for over five hundred years by characterizing Koreanism and producing the Hyun Mo Yang Cho ideal for setting the image and social roles of Korean women. It has been deeply embodied for so long in Korean cultural tradition, political behavior, family institution and educational system that the Korean people have all become "Confucian-minded." It has been the funda- mental and major source from which Korean society has drawn the principal guidelines for social relations and social conducts. Koreans still strongly believe in Confucian values, behave, think, and feel in Confucian ways, despite the fact that Koreans, particularly Korean-Americans and specifically Korean-American women, have experienced new social realities and such social changes as modernization, westernization, christianization, industrialization and immigration to the American socio-cultural setting.

The major premises for this paper are: a) Korean-American women struggle with conflicting pressures between two forces—to preserve Korean cultural heritage and traditional values on one hand, and to adapt to social changes for survival and mastery of a new socio-cultural environment on the other; b) Korean-American women experience discrepancies and incompatibility between traditional Korean women's roles defined by Hyun Mo Yang Cho ideals and desirable women's images demanded by the social reality of contemporary society: c) Korean-American women encounter a social reality posing direct pressures and immediate conditions for developing a new self-image for the ideal Korean-American woman: and d) Korean-American women realize that the self-image and social roles of the Hyun Mo Yang Cho ideal are inadequate in the changed socio-cultural environment of American society and inconsistent with the principles of the women's human rights movement. Thus this paper attempts to critically examine Hyun Mo Yang Cho idealism by presenting an overview of Confucian ideals that have nurtured Korean sexism. The paper is, however, ultimately concerned with the newly emerging ideals and images of Korean-American women.

II. Critical Interpretation of Confucius' Belief

Confucius (551-479 B.C.), the Chinese sage who originated Confucianism both as a religion and a socio-political philosophy, established an ethical and moral system to govern all social relations in family, community and society. He believed that the graded social relation is an ideal approach to the harmony and order of human society. He identified many hierarchical social relationships such as father and son, husband and wife, older brother or sister and younger brother or sister, older and younger people, man and woman, master and servant, ruler and subject, etc. He taught his followers that becoming a good father, son, wife, mother, brother, sister is the initial and essential step toward becoming a true human being and consequently toward becoming a good citizen and building a moral society.[1] Such hierarchical social relations and feudal approaches to an ideal society may reflect fundamental values that are subject to criticism and challenge from egalitarian and democratic idealists. Confucian culture therefore has been one of the major causes for the Korean women's human rights movement since the 1970s.[2]

Confucius' definition of a true human being and his theoretical context of humanities were mainly based on ascribed social roles such as father, mother, wife, son, brother and so on. He de-emphasized such values as the individual's efforts for self-fulfillment toward divine perfection, excellent performance of attained social roles for societal needs, and searching for an ultimate truth through metaphysical experiences. Thus, his conception of a man did not fully reflect a total person involved in various domains of life beyond the family context. For example, a Confucian woman is born to be a woman, not a human, to become a mother, wife, and daughter only, not an educator, philosopher, businessperson, government official, or the like. She is also born to be of submissive social status in the Confucian social order.

Confucian orientation with male preference and male centrism may be significantly related to the background of Confucius' birth and childhood. His father, 70 years old, and his mother, 18 years old, gave him birth through their extramarital union solely for the purpose of having a son. His father already had ten children—all, except one, a crippled son, were girls—before Confucius' birth.[3] He was virtually the only son to his mother, who became a widow when she was only twenty-one and Confucius was three. He himself had only one son and his son also had only one son. Confucius' negative perception and discriminating attitude about women may have contributed to the development of Confucian sexism. He treated women in friendly ways, but more as pets and not equal human beings. He believed that women were inherently inferior to men and incompetent to perform non-domestic activities.[4]

He presented a noble reason for ritual values,

especially for ancestor worship, and formulated a logical rationale for the positive impact of ritual activities on personal cultivation and social order.[5] Nevertheless, his ritual-loving character may be significantly related to his personal experiences pertaining to the loss of his own father during his early childhood, and his search for the whereabouts of his father's tomb because his mother kept it a secret.[6] In particular, he devoted himself to a three-year mourning period over his mother's death and restrained himself from all sensual activities during that time.[7] Raised by his widowed mother, Confucius, as her only son, may be expected to have had a deep emotional attachment to her. He had a natural motivation and socially acceptable purpose for practicing this three-year-long mourning period of devotion and ritual. Such traditional discipline is thought to have been beneficial to Confucius and his followers. However, it implies that the longer the period of devotional mourning and the more complete the form of ritual ceremonies, the harder and heavier they imposed service roles on their women. Women were not given the opportunity for instrumental roles in ritual life.

It may be significant to note that his aristocratic lifestyle was so extreme and his aesthetical taste was so fastidious that he did not take food, dress and mat unless they were in perfect and fresh condition. They may be the major reason why his wife ran away and eventually divorced him. His son, his grandson and his disciples of consecutive successive generations were all divorced. Even Mencius was separated.[8] Confucius' fourteen-year-long life of traveling, visiting feudal lords and seeking jobs may reveal clues leading one to suspect that his life was unstable, and to question the stability of his family life and his wife's marital life.[9]

Confucius' family roots in the ruling class, his strong elitism, aristocratism, and feudal belief have all been incorporated into Confucianism. Thus, Confucian ideology may represent idealism for the ruling class, but not for grassroot society. He identified intellectual people with the moral upper class and therefore legitimatized the influence of the ruling upper class on the other people.[10] His assumption was that the educated person as a moral man must realize his responsibility and duties over his inferiors in Confucian heirarchy, and inferiors must submit to such moral authority. Confucius himself admitted that there were very few, if any, except the Yu-Soon Moral Kings Era, who demonstrated the ideals of such moral authority.[11]

His emphasis on educational values regarding personal and moral cultivation and his moral-ethical approach to social orderings remained only as Confucian ideology of "false-consciousness" (in Karl Marx's term), since there has been a growing discrepancy between such ideals and the reality of Confucian societies. The Confucian reality stimulated educational needs for social mobility rather than for personal growth, and strengthened the male-authority of dictatorial behavior over all social relations. Thus, the social status of women became a double minority—sexually and socially—

in Confucian society. Although Confucius was in a true sense an anarchist who disapproved of strong governments for law enforcement or rigorous coercion,[12] his doctrines contributed to establishing strong govenments of totalitarian states. He did not give much thought to human dynamics and their impact on people with low status in the social heirarchy. His perspective on human dynamics was within the context of a static rather than changing society. There has been a growing gap between his socio-political ideology and the reality of social changes in today's society.

III. Confucianism of Korean Society

Confucianism is one of China's philosophies that has exercised a powerful influence for the past 2,500 years. It has been a live force shaping thoughts and behaviors not only for her own people in China, but also for her neighbors, particularly Korea. It has influenced the marriage institution, family structure, political culture, educational system and other social relations. It has been strongly perpetuated in all domains of Korean life as the mainstream of Korean culture, particularly since the Yi dynasty government (1392-1910) adopted it as a state religion. Among many results of its impact on Korean society are the development of kinship-based community and social relations, indoctrination of strong familism and the patriarchal family systems, institu-

71

tionalization of Confucian sexism, the so-called Hyun Mo Yang Cho ideal and Nam Jon Yu Bi virtue, and the promotion of educational competition for social mobility.

1) Kinship-based Community and Social Relation

The adoption of the Confucian social system has meant growth for Korean family structure in size. The Korean royal government granted official kin-names and land to families to encourage them to grow in number and settle in granted lands. The similar kin-name families promoted the consanguineous marriage in order to expand their lands as well as their socio-economic powers. These many different kin-name families constituted kinship-based communities and competed with each other in the struggle toward a central power monopoly. Thus, Confucian influence on Korean society contributed to societal disintegration, although it produced a monolithic culture and a homogeneous mentality.[13]

Each kinship-based community developed a kinship-oriented social relationship. All individual members of the community are related to each other within the kin-family framework and thus identified as uncle, aunt, etc., instead of as Mr. or Mrs. or Miss in the individual framework. It is therefore a Korean custom that a friend calls my father as his father, and a neighbor calls any elderly person on the street as grandmother or grandfather. An individual's name and particularly first-name calling are not practiced in traditional Korean society.

Giving a name to an individual at birth means designation or assigning a social rank in the kinship-oriented social structure. The name indicates the birthplace (Bon Kwan), birth order of the family members (Hang Ryul), and birth status (Sung). The social rank of the name defines location in the kinship community and prescribes conduct in social relations with other people.[14] Korean women were even excluded from being granted names of their own as they were confined to domestic life. They were simply called so-and-so's mother, or so-and-so's wife, or inside-person (An Sa Ram), house-person (Jib Sa Ram) or otherwise, after the name of the name of the resident house (e.g., Sa Im Dang Kim Ci), if she was from a Confucian Yang Ban family.[15]

2) Confucian Familism and Patriarchal Family Structure

The Confucian political culture strengthened the Korean family system by legitimatizing male-authority and institutionalizing a patriarchal family structure. The Confucian emphasis on the importance of family life for personal cultivation and social ordering nurtured the growth of stronger familism, particularly preserving such values as family ties, filial piety, family discipline through submission, obedience, sacrifice and loyalty to the patriarchal authority. Thus, members of the family placed first priority on family interests rather than personal needs. Although Confucian humanism says that "I" exists within "We," the individual "I" as a woman in

the Confucian family reality has been denied by
demanding of her a life-time of submission and
sacrifice. Since the individual's reputation is directly
related to a family background, all family members
undertake to strive for family reputation and power.
An individual's worth and dignity are measured on
the basis of family success, rather than individual
difference or accomplishment. This contributed to
the development of the Confucian marriage
system as a means of shifting one's social status.
Marrying into an influential kin-name family means
security, reputation and success for a Korean
woman.[16] Therefore the woman is willing to submit
to male authority and the patriarchal family system.
She surrenders herself as man's property. Marriage
for Confucian Korean women is therefore a transfer
from the father's territory and protection to that of
another male; it is the terminal station of her own life
rather than the commencement of self development.

3) Hyun Mo Yang Cho Ideal and Nam Jon Yu Bi Virtue

Monopolistic Confucian traditions of male centrism developed such inhumanitarian and discrimi-
natory doctrines as Hyun Mo Yang Cho is the ideal
image of the Korean woman; she is a submissive
wife and a sacrificial mother. The Nam Jon Yu Bi
belief originated from the Confucian concept of a
woman's inherent inferiority and incompetency, and
the confinement of the woman to lifetime sacrificial
service roles. Thus, the Confucian male-centered and

patriarchal family contributed to the socialization of woman as dependent on father before marriage, on husband after marriage, and on son after husband's death (so-called Sam Jong Ji Do). Her incompetencies were further nurtured through such life experiences and led to the loss of her own rights for decision-making, or practice of her own freedom and independent judgement without permission from male authority.[17]

Hyun Mo Yang Cho is a typical image of traditional sex-role stereotyping that is restricted to the domestic world. The marital life cycle for the woman is fixed with lifetime commitment to lengthy childbearing and child-rearing, without her own life, own identity, own voice and the experience of her human rights and freedom.

4) Confucian Aims of Korean Education

The Confucian civil examination and Confucian school system during the Yi dynasty increased the Confucian population and the Yang Ban ruling class. Admission to Confucian schools meant becoming a Confucianist and Confucian-conversion was the prerequisite to qualify for the Yang Ban class.[18] The Korean educational system has since served as a legitimate means for social mobility to shift social status rather than for personal cultivation to improve moral character. One's social status and reputation were significantly based on one's educational background in terms of the years of training and the reputation of the school. As Korean society grew stronger, educational values and heated educational competition increased, producing many successful individuals, but failing to achieve social harmony in successful group life.

Confucian culture discriminated against Korean women in the equal distribution of educational opportunities until the adoption of a modern educational system by the new Korean government was established in 1948. Athough the adoption of a modern educational system opened wide the educational opportunites for Korean women, women's college education serves Korean women to prepare them for marriage or to increase marital power in general. Korean women including college graduates are, for the most part, choosing marriage for their terminal station in the pursuance of life goals rather than as new departures for self-enrichment through both marital and other social life experiences. Marriage and career pursuits are thus becoming a matter of choice for Korean women as "either/or" rather than attempting "both." Marital status poses a handicap for further educational opportunities and work experiences, rather than being an asset for social credibility or self-fulfilling activities. Many college graduate women in Korean society thus remain unemployed and, if not, mostly employed in fields or at jobs irrelevant to their educational backgrounds and areas of interest.

The Charter of Korean National Education[19] states that Korean education aims at preserving Confucian culture on one hand and implanting Western philosophies such as democracy on the other. It conveys that Korean education is devoted to such mutually exclusive ideologies as non-egalitarian Confucianism and egalitarian democracy. Korean schools continues to stress the importance of Confucian values such as familism, filial piety, obedience, traditional values, conformity, loyalty, collectivity, and nationalism. Confucian political culture still dictates curriculum contents, instructional modes, student culture, and hierarchical relations between teacher and student. The practice of male authority is persistently reinforced and Hyun Mo Yang Cho idealism is indoctrinated through educational goals, instructional patterns, textbooks, extra-curricular activities, etc.[20]

Such Confucian-influencing education may discourage students from developing personal reasoning, critical thinking, objective attitudes, and innovative challenge, and may desensitize them with regard to individuality, human diversity, universalism, internationalism, horizontal social relationships, future-oriented perspectives, etc. Coeducational schools are not yet common practice as the Confucian sexist culture has been in favor of sexual segregation in the school system. The ideal product of the Confucian educational system may therefore be identified as the "most average man" because the ideal product is the one who conforms best to the societal norm; the norm may be defined as average behavior of standardized behavior of the society. The Confucian educational system does not encourage the production of "the best person," that is, an individual who realizes the best of his/her potentials through self-fulfillment toward divine perfection.

IV. The Social Reality of Korean-American Women

Korean-American women encounter a social reality that is greatly different from the Confucian society of Hyun Mo Yang Cho as discussed in the previous chapter. Peter Berger defines social reality as a social construct, including social structure and social systems, institutionalization and socialization, social roles and life situation as "taken-for-granted."[21] On the other hand, George Mead explains that self-consciousness or the self-product is the result of the incorporation of the given socio-cultural setting.[22] It is thus significantly related to social reality as "a relational reality." These two theoretical references confirm that the changed Korean-American woman's social reality directly corresponds to the changing of her social roles and self-images; the Hyun Mo Yang Cho ideal of the Confucian society is therefore not necessarily true for the Korean-American woman in American society. The changed or new social reality embodies the significant implication that the Korean-American woman may experience direct pressures and immediate conditions demanding different molds of ideal self-products.

The social reality of Korean-American women may be described as a social construct that refers to ubiquitous experiences with social changes that involved: a) demographic reality, b) industrialization, and c) the feminists' movement; the other, "the particular" social construct that refers to unique experiences with immigration life in the American socio-cultural setting. Korean-American women's immigration experiences are, as revealed through several studies on Korean-Americans, characterized as an unique pattern of their adjustment to such dualistic social conditions as: a) ethnic identity with both Koreanism and Americanism; b) a social system of both Korean ethnic community and American majority society; c) lifestyle of both traditional and contemporary modes; and d) ideological orientation with both persistent Confucianism and predominant Christianity.[23]

Such universal and particular characteristics of social construction constitute the social reality of Korean-American women and serve as the major impetus for affecting their Confucian mentality, shaping new forms of self-consciousness, encouraging the emergence of non-traditional self-products. New self-products that are adequate to the changed social reality and consistent with the principles of human rights are necessary to Korean-American women not only for their survival and mastery of the changed socio-cultural environment, but also for their self-realization and self-fulfillment.

1) The Universal Social Construction Serving as External Forces Changing Women's Social Roles and Images

a) Demographic reality changing women's marital life cycle:

Both American and Korean statistics show that traditional patterns are undergoing change; first, the compression of child-bearing years coupled with lengthened life; and second, the expansion of women's labor market forces combined with family responsibility. Longer life spans and shortened child-bearing years contribute to increasing women's leisure time and the growth of flexibility in their marital life cycles. Such demographic reality and the socio-economic reality of more demand for women's paid work participation have complemented each other. They have contributed to the institutionalization of the small, nuclear family structure as well. Thus growing numbers of women are no longer confined to the world of home, but encouraged to participate in the world of work. More and more women became free from lifetime service roles, and more and more they became familiar with the practice of instrumental roles outside of the domestic boundary. They became flexible enough to find and enjoy more leisure time for their own life enrichment.

b) *Industrialization and emerging new social status for the working woman:*

Unlike the traditional housewife, who performs unpaid, domestic work, the working woman (working mother) has emerged as a new symbol capable of changing social status for women. Industrial society has reinforced the work ethic as a powerful social norm and women's work experiences have returned practical rewards such as economic freedom, opportunity for individual expression, a sense of self-worth and deserved self-esteem and accessibility to the world beyond the domestic boundary. Particularly, paid work implies income, power and privilege in the highly developed industrial societies and commonly reflects educational background, competencies, self-discipline, success in competition, productivity and the like. Thus, more and more women develop their desires for higher and longer educational opportunities and their ambitions for better and more diversified work experiences. On the other hand, industrialized society has developed the perception of housewife status as a self-worthless, alienated social role, with low self-esteem, incompetency and disorientation from the future, etc.

The complex and changing social system, as result of industrialization along with the creation of a variety of occupational fields and diversification of labor, demands specialized expertise, explosion of knowledge, etc., all of which have stimulated women to meet the challenge for more education and non-traditional work. Industrialization developed societal institutions and strengthened the role of educational institutions to take over the major responsibilities of children's education from the mother's bosom and knees. Such division of work at the societal level has developed a variety of educational institutions (e.g., public and private schools, day-care centers, nursery schools, learning centers, and so on) that share in the mother's role pertaining to the educational and recreational needs of children. Joint responsibilities for child-rearing have broadened the mother's non-traditional social relations and social roles beyond domestic boundaries.[26]

In addition, industrial society has recognized specialization and expertise as valuable assets and authorized persons with such assets to exercise professional authority over all domains of social life. Particularly, the development of social welfare institutions received public sanction to professionally intervene in family and marital life through social service agencies, welfare programs and social work intervention. In other words, family and marital life has been exposed to such outsiders as family service experts, legal advisors, marriage counselors, domestic violence protection centers, home-maker services, paid baby-sitters, etc. The traditional family concealed family affairs and marital problems within its boundaries. That confined the wife to the most private zone of her husband's life. However, families in industrial societies began to share their domestic and marital burdens with others through a developing social service system. The family of industrial society is no longer a strictly a private zone, but a unit between the private and public zones. Such joint involvement in the traditionally private zone has sensitized women to feel unmet needs in their social conditions and to wish to perform better in social roles.[27]

Women's extended social life coincided with expanded leisure time, since the technological advancement revolutionalized the traditional patterns of housework and domestic management. Modernization and automatization for efficiency in the domestic system, including electronic household utilities, modern housing structure, instant food products, etc., have all contributed to reducing women's work at home and in the kitchen. In addition, the joint responsibility of husband and wife over household chores and child-rearing has become common practice. More men have come to accept ideologically (if not behaviorally) the joint responsibility to share housework and child care with women. Thus, women have been freed from prolonged domestic engagement and have become more and more flexible with regard to leisure time and doing their own things.[28]

c) *The feminist movement and the struggle for women's better self-images and improvement of women's social status:*

Today, such words as feminist, women's rights movement, women's liberation and the Equal Rights Amendment (ERA) are familiar not only to women but also to men, particularly those in

83

American society. There are two aspects of women-related issues and movements: first, there is the struggle of women to discover their own identities and to shape better self-images. Women exist in this world and in this time, but have lost their own identities and voices. Particularly, the Korean woman who has traditionally lived with secondary identity (e.g., so-and-so's mother or so-and-so's wife) and only for her husband's purpose and her family's interests. The culture—whether it be Eastern or Western—has not permitted women to accept or gratify their basic needs as human beings and to grow and fulfill their potentialities beyond sexual roles.[29]

Second, there is an effort to engage in the reexamination of the role of women in all spheres of life, and the relationship of men and women in all social, political, economic and cultural institutions. This effort is primarily aimed at the eradication of sex discrimination through attempting legislative, economic and educational reforms. Such efforts hold self-evident truths such as "all men and women are created equal; that among their rights are life, liberty and pursuit of happiness." (Excerpt from the Declaration of Sentiments of the 1848 Seneca Falls Woman's Rights Convention.)

Korean women's human rights movements have been growing firmer and more active, particularly since the 1970s. The Declaration made by the Organization for the Korean Family Law Reform for Korean Women (Bum Yu Sung Ga Jok Bup Gai Jung Chock Jin Hoe), with support from sixty other Korean women's organizations in 1973, articulates the social and legal status of Korean women today accuses the Confucian cultural structure and traditions that have the major responsibility for Korean sexism and sex discrimination under the law.[30] It cries out that Korean women are the victims of the Confucian social system which has denied them their basic needs as human beings, has deprived them of the opportunity to realize their potentialities, and has restricted their efforts to become free and complete persons.

As the women's rights movement has grown stronger and spread wider, an increasing number of women in both Korean and American societies have experienced awakened self-awareness and increased consciousness of the need for self-realization and self-fulfillment. More and more women are becoming independent, productive, competent, human beings who are struggling to mold self-images with deserved self-esteem and human dignity and worth.[31]

2)   The Particular Social Construction Serving as Internal Forces Changing Korean-American Women's Self-Consciousness and Mentality

According to survey findings that the author conducted for the study of the Korean-Americans' consciousness structure in 1982, Korean-Americans have been changed since their immigration and the present status of their consciousness and mentality shows tendencies such as: a) more positive attitude toward Americanization with continuing pride in

Korean ethnicity; b) no longer sojourner mentality but still strong attachment to Koreanism; c) greater sense of commitment to the American society, but prevailing feelings of alienation; d) adaption to the contemporary lifestyle, maintenance of traditional behaviors; e) stronger ties with ethnic social relations, but social distance from American social systems; f) liberalized paternal roles but strong conservative beliefs in women's sex-roles; and g) predominant Christian influence over individual Korean-American's life; but persistent Confucian dominance over Korean ethnic community life.[32]

The survey results confirm that Korean-American women are no longer in the same social reality as Hyun Mo Yang Cho Korean women because the Korean-American women's consciousness and mentality are the products of dualistic social environments such as the Korean ethnic community and the American majority society. The dualistic features of their social reality and their relational reality have implications for Korean-American women who are identified with double minority status both as ethnic and sexual minorities. They are overburdened with double social roles both in the traditional life at home and the ethnic community, and in the contemporary life at work and in American society; confused between the two mutually exclusive orientations of Confucianism and Christianity; and in conflict between two pressures—to preserve traditional values and cultural heritages on one hand and to change the traditional behaviors and adapt to the new social reality on the other hand. These implications convey that Korean-American women must necessarily mold new self-products that will be non-traditional but adequate and desirable for a changed social reality.

V. Conclusion: Toward New Self-Products for Korean-American Women's Ideal Self-Image

The major points discussed in the previous chapters may lead to the conclusion that the social reality of Korean-American women is not likely to foster only one mold as Hyun Mo Yang Cho, but to nurture multiple molds of self-products. This is the result of the acculturation process with social changes as well as the ethnicization process within the Amercan socio-cultural environment. As already studied by Korean-American social scientists, the typology of Korean-Americans identified four groups such as traditionalists, pluralists, integrationists, and isolationists on the basis of their degree and mode of American adjustment.[33] The same may be true for the general framework for the possible typology of Korean-American women's self-products. However, the typology of Korean-American women's self-products will be based on the degree and mode of the individual Korean-American woman's incorporation of "either/or" or "both"—the traditional and non-traditional patterns within herself. We suppose that the extremely traditional and the extremely non-traditional models for the ideal Korean-American woman's image are placed at the far right and far left respectively on the social continuum axis. We assume then that the nearer the right, the more traditional the self-image and social role patterns; and the closer toward the left, the more non-traditional.

The following diagram presents the theoretical models for typologizing the Korean-American women's self-products on the basis of the degree of internalization and the mode of practicing "either/or" or "both"—the traditional and non-traditional characteristics. The innovationists are those who are no longer traditional but non-traditional ideologically as well as behaviorally; the incorporationists are those who integrate within self the traditional and non-traditional attributes; the combinationists are those who are dualistic by practising both traditional and non-traditional patterns of behavior; and the preservationists are those who are always traditional ideologically and behaviorally.

Typology Model for
the Korean-American Women's Self-Products

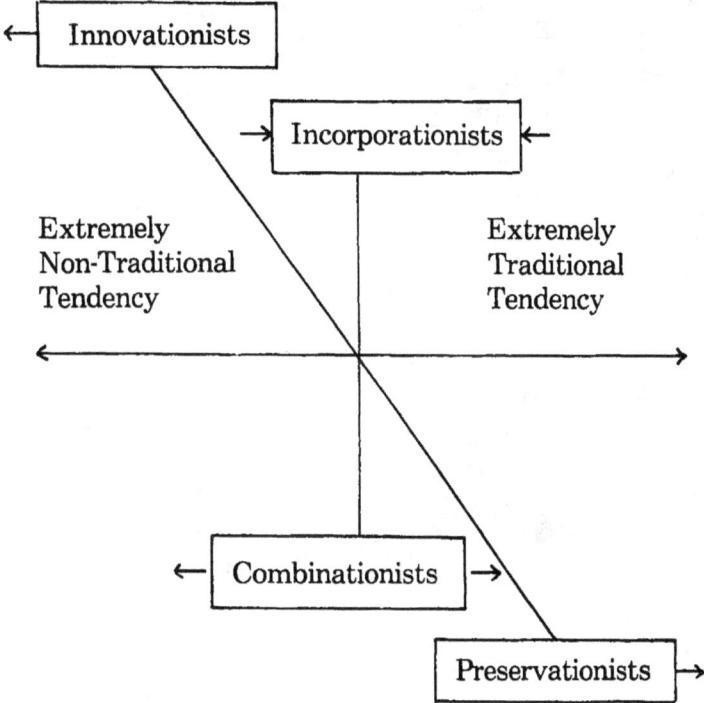

Innovationists

Incorporationists

Extremely
Non-Traditional
Tendency

Extremely
Traditional
Tendency

Combinationists

Preservationists

For the conceptual references for the typical and crucial differences between the traditional and non-traditional self-product model, the following chart is also provided.

Table 2 KOREAN-AMERICAN WOMEN'S SELF-PRODUCT MODE

	Variables	Traditional Model	Non-Traditional Model
a)	life goal-setting	to comply with traditional prescription	to satisfy with self-expectation
b)	control of behavior	tradition other-directed	principle self-directed
c)	ideal	Hyun-Mo-Yang-Cho (budget life for others)	self-fulfillment (budget life for self)
d)	marriage	life ends-goal graduation of own life	life means-goal commencement of own life
e)	life boundary	family and neighbor—confinement	family and society—extension
f)	major role	domestic, sexual expressive role	socio-economic and instrumental role
g)	social relation	static with people of homogeniety	dynamic with people of heterogeniety
h)	family relation	my existence for family life	family existence for my life
i)	dominant value	sacrifice, hierarchy (vertical relation)	freedom, equality (horizontal relation)
j)	identity	dependent identity A's wife or B's mother	independent identity, own identity

k)	self-concept	strong "we" weak "I"	strong "that's us!" strong "that's me!"
l)	individual character	with no personality	with personality
m)	motivation	selfishness of familism for bio-physical oneness	self-love of individualism for socio-moral oneness
n)	life satisfaction	from well-adaptation to the given life situation	from full-development of self
o)	marital relation	authoritarian-husband	companion-husband
p)	marital life-cycle	lengthy time for child- rearing and domestic chores	lengthy time for self-growth and development
q)	self experience	shame and guilt, low self-esteem	pride and confidence, deserved self-esteem
r)	role performance	negative, inadequate, social-dysfunctioning	positive, healthy, social-functioning
s)	impression	burden	role-model
t)	equal treatment	no recognition, no credit, no equality of results, sharing "consuming goods" of labor society	recognition, credit, equality of results, sharing "non- consuming knowlede" of information society
u)	life ultimate reality	to be separated from society and other human race	united to society and other human race

As the social psychologists (particularly the interactionalists) maintained, positive life experiences, desirable social relations, and successful social roles are all significant contributions to building positive self-esteem, adequate self-conception and desirable self-images. In other words, the self-conception about who I am, what I am and how I am is directly affected by whether or not my life experience was positive and if my social functioning was adequate. The underlying assumption of the changed social reality is therefore that self-products like Hyun Mo Yang Cho might have contributed to desirable self-concepts and high self-esteem for Koreans in such a static Confucian society, but the same may not necessarily be true for Korean-American women in a complex, changing society; or, that the self-product that emerges from pre-social changes might have led to an adequate self-image and positive social roles but the same is not consistently true for those that are emerging from the period of post-social changes.

Consequently, this paper is concerned with the social conditions and sociability of Korean-American women because they are the crucial subjects for determination of the adequacy and positiveness of their self-concepts and the fulfillment of their ideal self-images. This paper intends to suggest that the Hyun Mo Yang Cho model should not be practiced as a socio-cultural imposition, but as an alternative for optional choice by Korean-American individuals. This paper may, however, advocate that the traditional self-product of the Hyun Mo Yang Cho model is characterized by its "selfish lifestyle" to live only for "my husband, my children and my family," but the new ideal self-product is characterized by its "self-love lifestyle" to live not only for "my family and my community," but also for "our society and our human race."

Footnotes.

1. Lin Yutang, *The Wisdom of Confucius* (New York: The Modern Library, 1938, pp. 13-22.

2. Hyo-Jai Lee and Ju-Sook Kim, *(The Status of Korean Women* (Seoul, Korea: Ewha Woman's University Press, 1978, pp. 195-240.

3. Chiu Chai and Winberg Choi (eds.), *The Sacred Books of Confucius* (New York: University Books, 1965), pp. 18-21; Yutang, op. cit., pp. 55-57.

4. Miles Menender Dawson, *The Basic Teachings of Confucianism*, (New York: The New Home Library, 1942; Leonard Shiklieu Hsu, *The Political Philosophy of Confucianism* (London: George Routledge and Sons, Inc., 1932), p. 188.

5. Yutang, op, cit., p. 56

6. Ibid., p. 56

7. Chai and Choi, op. cit., pp. 20-23; Ibid., p. 57.

8. Yutang, op. cit., pp. 15-30.

9. Chai and Choi, op. cit., pp. 20-23; Hsu, op. cit., pp. 6-17.

10. Yutang, op. cit., pp. 22-23.

11. Ibid., p. 19.

12. Ibid., pp. 11-12; Hsu, op. cit., pp. 8013.

13. Tu-hon Kim,   (A Study of the Korean Family System), (Seoul, Korea: Uryu Mun Hwa Sa, 1949), pp. 128-130; Hyo-sok Kang, The Making of Confucian Society in Tokugawa Japan and Yi Korea: A comparative Analysis of the Behavior Patterns in Accepting the Foreign Ideology, Neo-Confucianism (Washington, D.C.: the American Univerity, 1971), pp. 102-107, p. 177.

14. Kim, op. cit., pp. 56-66.

15. Jae-suck Chai,   (The Social Characters of Korean People) (Seoul, Korea: Gae Moon Sa, 1983), pp. 27-42.

16. Kim, op. cit.,

17. Lee and Kim, op. cit., pp. 39-40; Soon-Man Rhim, "The Status of Women in Traditional Korean Society," Korean Women in a Struggle for Humanization, edited by Harold H. Sun Woo and Dong Soo Kim, Korean Christian Scholars Publication No. 3 (Spring 1978), pp. 11-37.

18. Kang, op. cit., p. 198.

19. Ministry of Culture and Information, Republic of Korea, Facts About Korea (Seoul, Korea: Korean

Information Service, 1982), p. 21.

20. Dug-Soo Son, *(The Status of Korean Women From the Perspective of the Women's Emancipation Movement)*, Sun-Woo and Kim (eds.), op. cit., pp. 257-272.

21. Peter Burger and Thomas Luckmann, *The Social Construction of Reality* (New York: Doubleday and Co., Inc., 1967).

22. George Mead, *Mind, Self, and Society* (Chicago: University of Chicago Press, 1934), pp. 164-194.

23. Won Mo Hurh, *Comparative Study of Korean Immigrants in the United States: A Typological Approach* (San Francisco: R and E Research Associates, Inc., 1977); Kwang Chung Kim, "An Exploratory Study of the Koreans in the United States: A Research Proposal," an unpublished working paper, 1972; Minza Kim Boo, " " (The Self-Consciousness of the Korean-American Women), Weekly News Paper, *Sae Gae Shin Bo* in New York, 12 series from January to March, 1982.

24. Janet Zollinger Giele, *Women and the Future: Changing Sex Roles in Modern America* (New York: the Free Press, 1975), pp. 160-178; Lee and Kim, op. cit., pp. 3-32.

25. Giele, op. cit., pp. 94-96.

26. Ibid., pp. 145-146.

27. John Romanyskn, *Social Welfare: Charity to Justice* (New York: Random House, Inc., 1971), pp. 333-335.

28. Alvin Toffler, *Future Shock* (New York: Random House, Inc., 1970)

29. Betty Friedan, *The Feminine Mystique* (New York: Dell Publishing Co., 1974).

30. Lee and Kim, op. cit., pp. 213-217.

31. Giele, op. cit., pp. 257-258.

32. Boo, op. cit.

33. Won Mo Hurh, "Toard a New Community and Identity: The Korean Ethnicity," *The Korean Immigrant in America*, edited by Byung-Suh Kim and Sang-Hyun Lee, Korean Christian Scholars Publication No. 5 (Spring 1980), pp. 1-25.

The Church and Feminist Theologies

Letty M. Russell

Introduction

Recently while lecturing in Japan a woman stood up and asked me whether it is possible to be a *Christian and a Feminist.*

Of course, I responded that it must be possible because I myself am very much committed to Christ. And I am also committed to working for the equality of women and men. This makes me a Christian and Feminist.

Today I would like to begin discussing *The Church and Feminist Theologies* by telling the story of how I came to be a Christian and Feminist. Then I will explain what feminist theologies are and how they contribute to both critique and renewal of the church.

Revision of a speech delivered for the NCC, Seoul, Korea, May, 1983.

I. BECOMING A CHRISTIAN AND FEMINIST

A. *My story of becoming a Christian and a Feminist begins when I was born.* And of course before, as we all have a family and cultural history. I was born into a Christian family and grew up as a Christian who trusted in the love of God in Jesus Christ. But I was also *born a misfit.* As a child I wanted to play active games and I was what they used to call a "Tom Boy." I refused to learn to read until I was in the fourth grade. I was taller than all the boys in seventh grade, and girls who are so tall—*don't fit* our stereotypes very well.

In college I joined the Student Christian Movement and responded to God's call to serve in the church. But when I told my father I wanted to be a church worker, he said, "You will always be a *misfit."*

And so I was. I was the first woman to enter Harvard Divinity School. I was one of the first women to be ordained in the United Presbyterian Church U.S.A. in 1958.

When I went to work as a white woman in a Black and Hispanic slum community in N.Y. I also thought I would not fit. But there I was welcomed by a community of misfits and oppressed people. There I learned that people are not misfits, because they have a problem. They are misfits because society is structured to keep them out of jobs and leadership roles because of their sex, race or class. I began to see that women become *misfits* whenever they assume that they are full human beings, and act as equal partners with men in church and society.

B. *Another aspect of my conversion story is my experience in the Civil rights movement in the 1960's.* While working as a pastor of an interracial and interdenominational church, I shared with my church members in advocating the change of laws, and the improvements of schools, housing, police protection, and civil rights.

Although I was white I could still work as an advocate for Black Liberation, and I saw this work as part of my Christian ministry. I believed that in God's sight no one is a misfit, for God intends us all to be full participants in the life of our community and nations. I worked to change the policies of the U.S. government that oppress people both at home and in other nations.

Gradually as I read the testimony of other women around the world. I began to realize that women too are often victims of social prejudice and discrimination. And thus I began to work for justice and human dignity for women and men. In short I was converted to human liberation. In this way I became not only a Christian, but a Feminist. I was committed to following the life style of Jesus Christ by serving all those whom are the outsiders or misfits in society. These are people Christ welcomed into God's kingdom.

II. DEVELOPING FEMINIST THOLOGIES

A. As a pastor and teacher I wanted to express my solidarity with women in my theology. *I began to write theology from the perspective of women struggling to be free*, so that both men and women can be more free.

Feminist theologies are different in different situations, cultures and traditions, but they share the ingredient of commitment or *advocacy of equality of the sexes*. Feminist theologies represent a search for liberation from all forms of dehumanization, by those who advocate full human personhood for all.

Feminist theologies are theology because the subject of reflection is God. All theology is thinking about God. What is *new* about them is that they take *women's experience* of God seriously in reflecting on how God is known to us.

Both men and women can be feminists and do feminist theology. The desire for equality in male and female roles needs to be and can be, shared and advocated by both men and women.

B. *Recently, I was lecturing on Feminist Theology in Japan and South Korea. When I said this, someone asked me if my husband was a feminist.* My husband, Hans Hoekendijk, was a Professor of Missions at Union Seminary in New York. He was hardly a likely candidate for feminism!

At first, he thought American women were very liberated in comparison to women in the Netherlands where he had lived before 1965.

101

But as he shared with me and with other women and men in the struggles to change the seminaries and churches he began to see that women are also very much 2nd class citizens in the U.S.

He shared with me in teaching, writing and in housework. His special task was washing the dishes. But, like most professors, he did not always pay attention to practical matters. One day he *forgot* to turn off the water and flooded the kitchen floor!

We each had our own name, but when I traveled with him for the YMCA in the US and Asia he was called Mr. Russell. When he traveled with me for the Dutch Mission Board, I was Ms. Hoekendijk. It did not matter to us because we were both equal persons with our own identities and thus could work as a team.

C. *Feminist theologies share the same style and method of theology as other of theology as other liberation theologies such as Minjung Theology in Korea*, L.A. Liberation Theology and Black Theology in the US and South Africa.

They begin with *commitment* to act on behalf of the oppressed and, they reflect on what this means in the light of God's liberating action in the Exodus and resurrection. You can not just *study* this theology. You have to *act* for the equality of women and men and then see what this means for your faith.

For example, many church women in the US have begun to respond to the increase of physical violence in the home, they are starting shelters for battered, and abused women and children. They also work to change laws that force women to remain as "property" of husbands who beat and abuse them. This has led to a reexamination of the biblical traditions that reinforce male domination and to social critique of the roots of violence in our society.

Secondly, these theologies are *contextual*. They begin in a concrete situation and ask about the problems and questions that arise in that context. The theological reflection seeks to be incarnated in the life, culture and social struggles of a particular people so that it can express God's presence in that place. This is why *for example* feminist theology in Korea can only be developed by Korean women together with other Asian women who share the same culture and social situation. The new *Stand* of the Korean Association of Women Theologians in establishing Asian Feminist Theology is an example of this. Meeting in a consultation in cooperation with Council of Churches in Asia, the reflected on their own history and set their own agenda. This agenda includes the democratizing of the Church community. It also calls for reinterpreting Korean culture in line with feminist theology. [Seoul, Feb. 1983, Consultation for the Establishment of Asian Feminist Theology]

Thirdly, feminist and liberation theologies are *collective*. Everyone is invited to take part. They invite the pastors, the lay people, activists, and teachers to reflect together on the work of the church in the world.

For example, in the United States small groups of

church women meet together in order to study the Bible and learn from each other. The Bible study I wrote recently for United Methodist Women on Ephesians was tested out by groups in the U.S. and Korea so that I could revise it in the light of contributions made by the participants, as a reflection on our collective insights and questions.

Lastly, feminist theologies like other liberation theologies seek to be *critical* theologies. They are experimental, trying to find the best questions for research, and questioning the contradictions they see in the church and society. Christian feminists join other oppressed groups in becoming critical of the action of the church in the light of the teachings of the Gospel. They test the tradition of the church and reinterpret biblical tradition in the light of the experience of women and all people struggling to be free.

For example, in the East Harlem Protestant Parish, where I was a pastor for many years, our Bible study made us critical of the injustice, racism and exploitation in our community and U.S. society. At the same time we shared in the Civil Rights Movement. We worked to integrate the schools, and develop a community organization to fight for better housing and police protection. This led us to be critical of the ways the Bible has been used to support oppression. We began to hear the word of God anew as a story of freedom for the oppressed at home and in other countries.

III. FEMINIST CRITIQUE AND RENEWAL OF THE CHURCH

A. *In the U.S., feminist theologians are contributing to the theology of the church in both critique and reconstruction of church tradition.*
Both women and men have developed a *critique* of the male bias of biblical and church historical tradition. They write about Bible, Church History, Theology, Ethics, and Pastoral Theology. In writing history of women in the church they point at their subordinate position in the organization of church life. At the same time they do research to *re-discover the history of women* that has been lost, because women's stories are seldom written down.
On the basis of this critique and new understanding of history women and men are able to *reconstruct theology as indigenous theology.* they work to create theology, such as my own, which reflects the meaning of the Christian faith from the perspective of women struggling to hear the Gospel in new ways. *Thus, for example,* new material on understanding of ordination has been developed out of the discussion of the ordination of women in preparation of Board of Education and Mission document and new approaches to Bible study from the perspective of the oppressed are developed.

B. *This critical perspective on church life can be an opportunity for renewal.* In asking new questions, and reflecting on their cultural perspective women and men in each nation and denomination have the possibility of developing theology in thier own context. I cannot say how that will develop for that is up to all of you each in your own context. I will only give you two examples of how feminist theologies promote church renewal in the U.S.

First, they help to *nurture the spiritual gifts of all the people* of God. Both women and men receive the gifts of the Holy Spirit. But often the gifts of women are not recognized, encouraged and used for the mission of the church. In keeping the women dominated and passive in the church the church itself remains weak. When women can share in leadership, preaching, evangelism and service the churches *double their potential for mission.*

Second, the recognition of the gifts of women has led to the discovery that *almost all lay people*, men as well as women, are oppressed in the church. The lay people are often submissive to the clergy and afraid to ask questions and proclaim the Gospel. They have been what are called the "frozen assets" of the church. This has led to critique of the structures of clergy domination and to more shared or team ministry.

For example, in East Harlem I worked on a team with the Secretary/Education worker and the janitor. In order for the secretary to become an educator and the janitor a spanish evangelist I did part of their jobs, running the mimeograph and sweeping the floor. In this way their talents multiplied so that we ended up with 3 ministers instead of one! I sometimes call this calculated inefficiency.

CONCLUSION:

I do not know what feminist theologies mean for the church in each part of the world, but I do know that they can make a very positive contribution to renewal and mission.

This will happen as women take the initiative. Working out their own theology. This theology would be based on the experiences and relationships of women and men in their social and political situation. It would not be based on some new form of continued U.S. imperialism.

I can only thank the women and men already at work in each area around the world, and continue to learn from the marvelously diverse Christian world community what this will mean!

Women's Emancipation Movement within the Christian Context.

Inn Sook Lee

Introduction

Tony Piantieri, my colleague and classmate, once poignantly pointed out during a graduate seminar that, theoretically, a woman can be elected president of the United States of America according to the present constitution, but she can not be elected priest.

The Judeo-Christian tradition, for thousands of years, has reflected the worldwide phenomenon of patriarchy. The ancient Biblical society featured the steady milieu of patriarchal culture, and the church has adopted a male dominant interpretation of religion by its close relationship with the prevailing culture.

While the New Testament is the greatest liberation story ever told, and while the gospel affirms that Christians have the responsibility to transform the culture which poses its hierarchically ordered value systems as ultimate, yet the Christian tradition and Christian church structure have continually maintained the very social values and customs of society.

The Women in the church, yearning to be freed from the ongoing bondage and historical condition of negation and exclusion, and yearning to affirm their authentic humanity and full partnership in mission, have led courageous movements to raise feminist critical consciousness. Women, in spite of the harshness of the power system under which they suffer, have been suggesting, for thousands of years, an alternative vision as a metaphor of their ongoing struggle for humanization. The records of women's appropriation of the good news and the Women's emancipation movement are evident generation after generation.

The words spoken two thousand years ago by a chorus of women in Euripides' Medea (Carol P. Christ and Judith Plaskow, 1979) lauding for spiritual quest for women based on women's experience, to the words written by contemporary thinkers, are illustrations of the pursuit of feminist spirituality, Christian identity and women's appropriation for full humanity.

The 17th century scriptural exegesis of Margaret Fell asserts that "women's preaching" was "justified according to the Scriptures," and the writings of the Enlightenment movement are good examples, traces of which were seen more clearly in the writings of the Women's movement in the 19th century.

Biblical commentaries and essays written since the 18th century reveal traces of different ways of understanding the Biblical material. By the mid 20th century, Protestant churches in the United

States began to accept women students in seminaries—(e.g., Harvard Divinity School in 1955 -Hageman, 1974), and started to ordain women ministers shortly thereafter (Verdesi, 1973). Even though women have achieved legal rights to ordination in some protestant churches, the issues of placement and psychological well-being in job situations call for greater improvement.

In 1933, women in the Presbyterian Church in Korea demanded eldership in the church structure by submitting a petition signed by 150 women to the General Assembly. However the legislation was rejected. The Assembly over-ruled the request saying that it was too premature. In 1934, 537 women from 22 churches in the Hamnam Presbytery signed the petition and demanded the ordination of women, and the issue was enlarged to the question of the authority of the Bible, brought to a lawsuit and was withdrawn (Kim, 1976).

During the 1984 General Assembly of the Presbyterian Church in the Republic of Korea, the same legislation was again defeated by the margin of 50/50 (GA Report, PC ROK, 1984). Even though it is a clearly known factor that in Asian social and Christian culture, the suppression of women is great, the church leaders have come to realize, once again, the depth and strength of male domination in the contemporary Korean Christian milieu.

The bottom line of culturally bound ideology still seems to be that women are expected to stay home to carry on domestic duties, to marry and bear children, especially males. They have been unknowingly kept in bondage through economic disadvantage, and through cultural, moral and religious education which society has continually imposed on them. Women have been scolded, even verbally assaulted for having intellectual ideas, standing on certain issues, and being active in society. Ongoing women's experience of exclusion makes us critically aware that women are expected to stay comfortably in the position of a less than human, ignoring the genuine possibility of becoming full and authentic human persons.

The culturally bound idea of suppression of women is strongly operative in the Church in Korea as well as in the Korean-American immigrant community. In spite of the fact that the Protestant Church in Korea and in Korean immigrant community is the fastest growing church in the world, and 68 percent of the church constituency is reported to be women (The Christian Herald, 9/26/84), women are kept in the position of subordination in the Church structure. Women are allowed to serve neither as elders nor as ministers in many denominations.

Since the early 1970's, many feminist Christians, worldwide, women and men alike, joined in a prophetic movement of feminism, which arose as critiques of culture in the light of patriarchal oppression of women, demanding re-examination of Biblical material, proclaiming human dignity for women, and started a praxis of self-initiated, self-creating, intentionally and reflectively enacted activities of human emancipation.

Many thinkers from the Judeo-Christian tradition

111

joined the longest revolutionary movement, and called for a search for a new paradigm in Christian community in which the radical love of Jesus Christ can be exercised in reality. They proclaimed the Gospel for all people, rich or poor, oppressed and oppressors and women or men. They called for the affirmation and promotion of authentic full humanity for women which is the inclusive humanity, centered around the imago dei, the paradigm of Jesus Christ.

Some leading theologians proclaimed the transformation of gender biased religion into creating a new community where the gifts of holy spirit bestowed for all and felt by all (Daly, 1974, Ruether, 1983). They are hoping for the new humanity where the apocalyptic community is possible in which roles will no longer be assigned on the basis of gender but on the variety of non anatomically determined gifts, and rejoicing and celebrating the gift of life, to receive, to live and to pass on, for all people in its full humanity (Sargent, 1977). They would regard the action as a participatory act in the restoration of the meaning of God's original intentions for creation.

The goal of this essay is to observe the directions and options taken by some women scholars in the contemporary Christian context, on the women's emancipation movement, calling for the consciousness, human dignity and a community of justice.

Directions Taken in the Women's Movement.

Many contemporary Christian scholars who are teaching in the academic institutions have published a considerable amount of resource material on the subject area of women's human liberation. Christian feminists, especially those in the biblical field, point to various cases of ancient biblical prophets re-interpreting the scriptural material, relating to the people of their time. The scriptures show that one of the major responsibilities the prophets performed was critiquing the prevailing culture and the authorities who were exercising power in the system (Sakenfeld, 1975).

The scholars who are working toward the search of truth and working against the unjustified negation and exclusion of women seem determined to work within the Christian religious heritage. They intend to address themselves to the authority of the Bible (Fiorenza, 1983, Ruether, 1983) in the life of the community of faith. Believing that the Bible has been pervasively influential in sustaining patriarchy in the faith community, the scholars recall ignored verses and reinterpret biblical traditions as they search for a new paradigm within the belief community.

Three major approaches can be identified in reading the resource material in the new interpretation of the Bible and of the Christian tradition. They are:

1. The Struggle for Consciousness: Biblical Reinterpretation Approach.

2. The Struggle for Human Dignity: Liberation Perspective Approach.
3. Searching for a New Paradigm within the Christian Community.

These options neither seem to occur exclusively of each other, nor seem to occur chronologically. Many essays, in fact, seem to combine these approaches in the dialogue with the Bible and with the Christian tradition. The purpose of delineating simply is to sharpen our understanding of the ongoing struggle with the biblical text and the tradition of the church community.

I. The Struggle for Consciousness: Biblical Reinterpretation Approach.

Acknowledging the androcentric principles that are deeply imbedded in Christian reality, biblical scholars also recognize the composition of the Bible by men writers and its interpretation done by men from a patriarchal perspective. Some contemporary scholars are actively searching for effective and usable interpretative methods that are workable for the new egalitarian hermeneutics.

The approaches the biblical scholars take seem to be three-fold.

a). Reinterpretation of the texts that are "against" women.

b). Highlighting the biblical texts that affirm the full humanity of women.

c). Understanding the issue in light of cultural and historical perspectives.

1. a). Reinterpretation of the texts that are "against" women.

Many androcentric leaders in the Christian tradition point to the Bible as the guide for maintaining patriarchy in the system. Some of the most common texts and traditions used for this purpose include the themes that woman was created second (Gen. 2) and sinned first (Gen. 3), women were to keep silent in church (1 Cor. 14) and to be submissive to their husbands (Eph. 5) (Trible, 1973. Sakenfeld, 1975. Fiorenza, 1983.) These have been the controlling passages of the Scriptures concerning women, in the Christian tradition, for over two thousand years. Many scholars feel that these views reflect the culturally-bound and culturally biased ideas that have permeated church culture. These hierarchical views are still being exercised in church communities in many parts of the world.

In an effort to reinterpret some of the passages, biblical scholars point to the theme of "woman sinned first" that although the serpent addresses the woman, the Hebrew texts make it clear that the man and the woman were standing "together" during this encounter (Sakenfeld, 1975). An Old Testament scholar, Katharine Sakenfeld, points out that all of the you verbs in this encounter are plural in the Hebrew narrative. She writes that some ancient versions read, "and they ate" which depicts even more a joint action. The observations picture clearly that the man was there the whole time, and simply took the fruit without a question or objection. Their eyes were opened at the same time, together they made aprons, and together they hid from God. Further, the judgement came equally upon the woman and the man.

The narrator observes the joint action of disobedience of the man and the woman. Sakenfeld observes, from the above narrative, that it is remarkable that in a strongly patriarchal ancient society, such as in the Palestine-Judeo society two thousand years ago, such a good narrative with the idea of human equality was even thought of. She contends that the narrator saw the goodness and blessing of God, and that the subordinate role of women in culture was not ordained by God, but a result of human rebellion.

Many biblical scholars such as Katherine and Richard Kroeger observe that Corinth was not an ordinary city. They designate the city as the most licentious city in the world at that time. They point out that there were many Gnostics, in the city of Corinth, who go in to a trance, dancing and yelling during their worship services. Many did not want them in church during this period of establishing the church in the name of the new prophet Jesus of Nazareth. But the Apostle Paul wanted to include everyone. Many scholars believe that the Apostle

Paul was addressing this particular group to be silent during worship service in church (1. Cor. 14:11) noticing their trance and yelling in the aisles of the sanctuary in the middle of Christian worship service.

Researchers contend that the Apostle Paul's infamous command, which generated the continued victimization of women for many decades, was not addressed to all the women in the Christian church structure, but to a particular group of women in a particular circumstance.

A husband and wife team, the Kroegers, interpret "the submission" in Ephesians Chapter 5, as mutuality and commitment rather than a servant-master relationship. The extended passage the verse 21, clearly depict the meaning of mutuality when it says "submit to one another." This passage in being re-interpreted by biblical scholars as mutuality and reciprocity to one another as with Christ's self-sacrificing love and care are to be emulated by us all believers, for and to one another, especially between husband and wife.

1. b). Highlighting the biblical texts that affirm the full humanity of women.

Another way of seeing the reality is the egalitarian perspective. The egalitarian view sees woman as a complementary partner to man in creation, ontologically and functionally equal to him. Genesis 1, the life of Jesus, Galatians 3:27-28 and Ephesians 5:21 have become the controlling Scriptural passages for this view. Many Christian commentators and theologians seem to interact with specific elements in different ways within the egalitarian model and the model seems to be widely accepted. Beyond its support from Scripture, the new pattern is supported by the shifting roles of women in western culture with their social, psychological, educational and legal changes, affecting the role of women in society.

The additional biblical foundations for establishing the egalitarian model are the female prophetic tradition in Isreal and the Church, the affirmation of women by Jesus Christ, regarding them as whole and thinking human beings, the status and the ministry of women in the Early Church, and the teachings of Apostles Paul and Peter.

An Old Testament scholar, Phyllis Trible, suggests a new understanding of the creation story. The close interpretation points out the redaction based on Gen. 1 in which it says God created humankind in God's own image, in the image of God, created male and female, and God blessed them and said to them to have dominion over every living thing that moves upon the earth (27-28). She explains that it is immediately clear that male and female are created together and equally in the image of God. She eloquently points out that, in this creation redaction, there is no subordination expressed or implied. It is seen clearly in this chapter, God "created them" together, in God's own image, "blessed them" together, equally to "have dominion", and God pronounced "very good."

It is clearly shown that God's intention for men and women was a complementary partnership, as they are created equally in the image of God, jointly given the charge to be fruitful and to have dominion.

Genesis 1, also reads, that God created woman as a helper for man. Many bible readers notice plainly that the term translated as "helper" is used so often of God in the Old Testament, consequently, the new interpreters conclude that no secondary position for woman, as man's helper, seems to be required by the text. The focus of the passage is that man exults toward the creation of woman saying, "bone of my bones and flesh of my flesh," pointing to the similarity and the unity. God's act of creating one like man seems to stress complementarity, companionship, and interdependence.

The long tradition of women prophets in Israel—Sarah, Miriam, Deborah, Hulda, Esther and Anna—points to the age when the spirit was poured out on all of God's people. The priesthood finds its fulfillment in the High priest, Jesus Christ, and becomes the priesthood of all people of God, female and male.

So much has been written about Jesus and his support for women. Jesus regarded, accepted and supported women as whole, thinking and independent human beings, going against the Palestinian tradition in which the suppression of women was great. He did many things to liberate them from unjust oppression, negation and exclusion.

The status of women in Palestinian Judaism during the time of Jesus had become far more restricted than it was in the earlier Old Testament period (Trible, 1973). But, Jesus supported Mary of Bethany studying the Scripture when the prevailing teaching of the "Torah", the people's bible, was to "burn the Torah instead of teaching it to women." He commissioned a woman, Mary of Magda, to tell the good news of the resurrection when women were not even allowed to be witnesses in human courts of justice.

A rabbi was not to speak with a woman in public. Women were not to participate aloud in any public worship, they did not count toward the necessary quorum of ten for Synagogue worship. And there were countless number of laws, restricting, and dehumanizing women. The poignant story of Jesus' conversion conversation with the nameless woman of Samaria stunned even his own disciples. The Scripture reads the disciples were stunned and dumbfounded when they saw Jesus speaking with a Samaritan woman. This was the longest recorded conversation ever to appear in the Scripture. He regarded her as a thinking human being, leading the theological conversation with her. Jesus made a nameless sinful gentile woman his first woman evangelist. He announced his messiahship to this very woman, the symbolic outcast of society.

Many scholars believe that Jesus' attitude toward the women of the time, and choosing them to reveal his identity and to carry out the one of the most important messages in his ministry of servanthood was his deliberate choice to free women from their oppression and subordinate status. He revealed his messiahship to "the woman at the well", he revealed himself being "the resurrection and the life", and being "the son of God" to Martha of Bethany. He also commissioned Mary of Magda to spread the news of his resurrection, one of the most important events in Christian belief.

Many feminist scholars believe that Jesus was a radical liberator (Swidler, 1979). His attitude was remarkable considering the culture in which he was brought up. It is even astonishing and revolutionary for his time. He inaugurated the new world just the way God had intended (Sakenfeld, 1975). His efforts to restore a graceful and transcending world of God where both men and women can be free and wholesome humankind was seen clearly in his ministry.

The Apostle Paul has to be interpreted in light of Galatians 3:28 (Fiorenza, 1973) where it says "For as many of you were baptized into Christ, and have put on Christ, there is neither Jew nor Greek, there is neither slave nor free, there is neither male nor female; for you are all one in Christ Jesus." Many Christian scholars ground their view of women's place in family, society, and church on this text. The Apostle was proclaiming that the value judgments based on race, gender, and class are set aside in Christ Jesus. Apostle Paul envisioned the restoration of equality between Jews and Gentiles. He envisioned the restoration of equality between male and female, the kingdom already inaugurated by Jesus Christ.

Because of the influences from Jesus and Paul, the atmosphere in the early church was relatively open.

Women had full participation in the Upper Room. Dorcas was called a disciple, and had an active ministry (Acts. 9). Priscilla was a teacher of Apollo and had ministered to Gentiles (Acts. 18). Philip's two daughters were given full leadership and authority. Phoebe was given full authority, was sent to Rome on church business with decision making authority, and was called a minister (Rom. 16). Many women in Apostle Paul's ministry were referred to as fellow laborers and co-workers. They were entrusted with greater responsibility and sense of importance in the church, thus in society.

Apostle Paul's battle against the circumcisors in Galatia not only maintained the gospel of God's grace but also an equal place for women stressing the centrality of baptism, as members of the gospel community, as demonstrated in each and every Christian baptism. The prophets, after the earthly life of Jesus, worked in the time of eschatological tension. They believed the end was near, thus feeling an urgency in spreading the gospel, and at the same time, had to support women, going against the societal trend. Considering the tension filled situation, Apostle Paul's support for women church workers in the early church is remarkable.

I. c.) Understanding the issue in light of historical and cultural perspective.

Anthropologists Bachofen tells us that matriarchal system was exercised during the ancient prehistoric farming age. The system was influenced by the ideology based on the productive and reproductive spheres of natural abilities. The historian Engels writes in his book *The Origin and History of the Family, Private Property and the State* that during this ancient prehistoric age, they worshiped Goddesses and the Mother of the Universe. The change gradually took place as men came to exercise their superior physical strength over women. As the system of monogamy began to be introduced to the prevailing social system, the oppression of women started to appear as well.

During the first century, as Christianity spread throughout the Gentile world, a pro-Greek trend quickly developed. Inspite of the clear attitude of support of women expressed by Jesus and by some of the Pauline writings, Christianity's choice went to the anti-feminine Pauline and deutero-Pauline writings (Swidler, 1979). Apparently the rigid patriarchal social system was so pervasive in the lives of the majority of Christians that they did not pay much attention to the new alternative, and gravitated toward the most restrictive subordinationist passages of the New Testament.

A historical theologian Elisabeth Schüssler Fiorenza depicts clearly in her new book *In Memory of Her* that the Jesus movement was a reform movement within Judaism, characterized by an inclusive vision of the Kingdom, by the praxis of the discipleship of equals. According to the gospels of Mark and John, even the pre-Pauline Christian missionary movement was marked by the apostolic and ministerial leadership of women. Fiorenza contends that the gradual formation of the patriarchal church and the elimination of women from church leadership in the post-Pauline and post-Petrine period, was largely for apologetic reasons. Thus during the second century the shift occurs from charismatic and communal influence to authority vested in the patriarchal house of God.

New Testament scholars further explain that in the first century, Christianity was so intent in differentiating itself from the world around it that in an effort to establish an identity it often vigorously rejected the Hellenistic and Gnostic worlds. They contend that the Hellenistic world included a relatively high status and activities for women (Swidler, 1979.)

The third historical element can be that when the second generation Christians were forming the Church structure, they had adopted a Greco-Roman model, e.g., diocese, parish, originally Roman civil administrative terms, which almost entirely excluded women (Swidler, 1979). To all of these, the pervasive Greek ideology of dualism was added during the period of the Middle Ages.

Dualism, in short, is a theory that considers reality consisting of two irreducible modes, the opposing principles one of which is usually regarded as superior to the other; such as heaven versus earth, day versus night. It compared men with spirituality and considered them superior, and women with earth and materialistic elements and considered them inferior (Britannica encyclopedia, 1984). This ideology perpetuated the hierarchical mode which had influence on the oppression of all voiceless groups.

Some biblical scholars find themselves engaged in prooftexting and find strong systematic pervasiveness of patriarchy in the Bible. They feel that the patriarchy in the church structure will not be undone in their lifetime or the coming generations, and feel that attention to the Bible seems futile. Others seem to feel, precisely for this reason, that they need to strongly highlight the intentions of God and Jesus expressed in many ways in the Bible.

II. The Struggle for Human Dignity: The Liberation Perspective Approach.

Another approach the interpreters use is the approach of liberation perspective. These particular theologians are seeking to rediscover God's compassion and concern for the oppressed and the poor, thus God's original intentions for women and their status.

Liberation interpreters seek to highlight the liberation themes that are strongly pre-existent throughout the Bible. They are searching for a hermeneutics that is rooted in the feminist critical consciousness that women and men are fully human and fully equal. Many women and men are struggling to find an egalitarian consciousness and serious consideration of the biblical witness to the story of God's equal presence in the lives of women and men.

The new hermeneutics embrace a variety of meth-

odologies and disciplines. Some theological interpreters feel that feminist theology and hermeneutics
should draw upon women's experience as a basis for
their theology just as human experience is a base for
the traditional theology, and just as black experience is a basis for black theology. They feel that
only human experience at its deepest level can provide the power and the profound yearning for deeper
meaning and better understanding of human life on
this earth.

In order to find God's concern and to seek the central witness of the scriptures, liberation interpreters
turn to the deeds and words of Jesus Christ, the in-
carnate word of God. They try to search for the
world of God of freedom through the world made
known in the Jesus of Nazareth. Their efforts
toward seeking freedom and equality tend to place
feminist hermeneutics within the larger context of
liberation theology.

Letty Russell, a theologian who has persistently
been working for the freedom of humanity from all
forms of bondage—racism, sexism, classism—emphasizes the perspectives and themes which may
relate to the liberating core of the Christian faith.
She turns to themes such as "hope in freedom of
God", Jesus Christ as "representation of humanity"
and as "a unique revelation of true personhood."
(1974). To emphasize her yearning for freedom and
humanity for all, she quotes Moltmann's writings in
religion saying "We are saved in hope which comes
from having already tasted of the firstfruits of the
Spirit of freedom. Insofar as we have a small foretaste

of God's gift of freedom, we are also led to see more clearly that this gift is intended by God for all women and men." (1974).

She also writes in her infamous book *Human Liberation* that "The main clue that we have as Christians beyond this foretaste which both judges and comforts us is that of Jesus of Nazareth. In him we trust that God has made known the beginnings of the love, obedience, and true humanity,.......Jesus embodies in his life, death, and resurrection what a truly human being might be like. One who would love and live and suffer for love of God and for others." (pp. 34).

She shows much understanding and compassion for the people from the Third World. She continues to write in *Human Liberation* that "Inspite of the gospel of liberation and the words and actions of Jesus, the church has too long supported the idea that non-whites, non-westerners, and non-males are slightly less than human. . . .The Third World people in the United States, are not just separate ethnic groups, but "inferior human beings" with low status. The same dynamics are operative in relation to women....Caste is often even more insidious and dehumanizing than class because it is almost impossible to overcome one's sex or the color of one's skin."

Russell proclaims "the hope of change" in the "act of proleptic action of breaking bread" together in communion as a community which crosses racial, sexual, class, and national lines (1974). She focuses explicitly on God in Christ as the basis for

127

hope of humanization. Searching for humanity and human nurture, in the word of shalom, wholeness or salvation encompasses all people in all conditions of life. This ideology provides the norm affirming the solidarity of God in human suffering and God's negation of the unfreedom of today. This ideology also provides the basis for the solidarity of the whole human community as people of God in one egalitarian community and as the hope for the future.

In the same liberation theme, Rosemary Ruether proclaims, in her recent book *Sexism* and *God-Talk*, the prophetic principle of rejection of any elevation of one social group against the other, posing as the image of God or an agent of God. She also rejects every use of God to justify the present unjust social order, social domination and subjugation. She asserts, in her book, the affirmation and promotion of the full humanity of women. She writes, "whatever denies, diminishes or distorts the full humanity of women is to be appraised as not redemptive and must be presumed not to reflect the divine, nor to be the work of an authentic redeemer, nor a community of redemption." (1983).

Ruether also asserts that the women's on-going dehumanizing experience of sexism in the androcentric, patriarchal society should be the hermeneutical key for feminist theology, just as the Exodus experience and the resurrection experience are the primary data for the traditional theology and religion. Although there might be cross-cultural differences of the experience of sexism, she contends, that the hope of overcoming oppression can only begin when women become freed and empowered to critique the women's experience as an unjustified assault upon their beings.

Rosemary Radford Ruether, Letty M. Russell and Elisabeth Schüssler Fiorenza along with others are hard at work in the construction of feminist theology including Christology and Mariology as symbolic Ecclesiology. Liberation Mariology is endearing many who read it as the church as humanity redeemed from sexism. Ruether asserts that Luke, the physician author of the Gospel Luke, goes out of his way to stress that Mary's mother-hood was a free choice of her own. Ruether's inter-pretation is that when the angel arrived, Mary does not consult Joseph, but makes her own decision. Feminist Luke sees this as free choice of her own, made as an expression of her deep faith in God. An unwed mother, at the time, was put to death by human courts. Mary had deep trust and faith in God, enough to risk her own life to cooperate with God's plans to redeem this world.

The critique of sexism in contemporary and his-torical Christian culture as patriarchal, and the con-struction and interpretation of religion done by men from a patriarchal perspective include elimination of traces of female experience in that religion. Ruether talks much about the tradition having been shaped and excluding women, and the tradition having been shaped to justify their exclusion. She writes "the traces of their (women's) presence have been sup-pressed and lost from the public memory of the community. The androcentric bias of the male interpreters of the tradition, who regard maleness as normative humanity, not only erase women's presence in the past history of the community, but silence even the question about their absence. One is not even able to remark upon or notice women's absence, since women's silence and absence is normative." (1983).

Elisabeth Schüssler Fiorenza talks on the same theme in her recent publication *In Memory of Her* that the name of the faithful disciple the woman who anointed Jesus during Jesus' last days on earth, was erased or virtually forgotten because she was a woman.

Fiorenza explains, in the passion account of Mark's Gospel, that Judas who betrays Jesus and Peter who denies him are recorded and remembered, but the one who performed a prophetic sign-action of anointing Jesus, the one who had the prophetic knowledge of Jesus's death, the one who had enough love and courage to carry out the action of buying the expensive oil and go to men's group to empty herself enough to wash Jesus' feet with her hair which was a symbol of dignity and honor for women at the time, did not become a part of the gospel knowledge of Christians. Although Jesus himself pronounces in the Gospel Mark "And truly I say to you, wherever the gospel is preached in the whole world, what she has done will be told in memory of her" (14:9), her name is lost to us because she was a woman.

Rosemary Radford Ruether talks about women's experience of negation and trivialization put upon their biological characteristics and presence. Women's experience of birthing and nurturing other human beings are used to justify their exclusion from cultural opportunities and leadership. Their biological presence is regarded as a threat to male purity, and become subject to verbal and physical abuse and assault.

Ruether strongly contends that women's biological difference and those very functions should be brought to the hermeneutical task. She proclaims that women's expereince of birthing and nurturing may be used as paradigms of divine-human relationships. They should affirm their own bodily experience as good and normative, and they should judge their own biological experience as their own authentic humanity, thus progressively free themselves from the culture that negates them. She eloquently preaches the need for constant reevaluation of biblical tradition, and the need for a constant search for the truly liberating meaning of the Word of God.

Scholars who incline toward this approach are first to admit the seriousness of patriarchal infusion in the Bible. But their firm theological belief seems to be that there is timeless truth to be identified in the Scriptures, their efforts to identify the culturally conditioned parts of the Bible is an effort to discover that timeless truth.

III. Searching for a New Paradigm within the Christian Community

Many church leaders are looking for a new egalitarian paradigm where each person becomes an authentic human in a new community.

Elisabeth Moltmann, wife of the famous German theologian Jurgen Moltmann, eloquently voiced her conviction on the subject of church and women during a consultation that church history began when a few women set out to pay their respects to their dead friend Jesus on Easter morning. It began when a few women did what they considered to be right. They treasured the principles of equality of life Jesus taught them. She further explains that church history began when Jesus came to them after his resurrection and restored them (Thompson, 1982.)

But Moltmann notes that this Matthew account of the Easter appearance has never been known as the beginning of church history, but it began when all men system officially took over the apostolic succession. She contends they reign, judge and govern. Their image of God as male leadership which corresponds to what they would like to be—judge, king, ruler, army commander. In the process, she explained, women's experiences of Jesus have been forgotten—the one who is friend, who shares their lives, offers warmth and tenderness in their loneliness and powerlessness.

Jurgen Moltmann proclaims that God is not on the side of the patriarchate, and Christianity did not introduce the patriarchate into the world. He argues that Christianity proved inadequate in opposing the ancient and widespread system of male domination and soon found itself taken over by men and serving the system.

Moltmann strongly asserts the need for men to be delivered from the distortion of suppression. Men have been taught to adopt the role of trained soldier, conqueror, ruler, breadwinner and they are ruled by the anxiety to make something of themselves. He argues that man is far from benefitting from the patriarchate in his emotional life, but is cut in half into a subject of reason and will, an object of heart, and feelings. A woman is divided into images of mother and wife also, and has no image of personhood of her own. This narrowed down, oppressive image and system induced to produce unresolved mother fixations and machismo against other women (Thompson, 1982).

We need to transform the image of the lonely majesty of the God of heaven, all powerful, incapable of being influenced or of suffering. We need to discover the warm image of Jesus' Abba who reaches to the depths of our souls, the one who dwells in our daily lives suffering with us, and the one who lives in our community redeeming us from our inequities.

Church leaders talk about the change from a pyramid system to the community of a circle. Many in the church structure are blinded by the notion of power and control which is their image of masculine kingdom.

Dr. Philip Potter, former general secretary of the World Council of Churches, eloquently asserted during a conference in England the need to rethink the question of authority and power exercised in the church structure. He confessed honestly that we systematically set aside the central nature of God's revelation and set aside the insight and wisdom of women lying there wasted for so many years, and clung to all things that confirm and strengthen our attitudes of domination and of hierarchical oppression. He continued to say that ministry means being the servant, one who empties him or herself, instead of seeking to have power and domination.

Letty Russell asserts in her much admired book *The Future of Partnership* that the basic qualities considered important for true partnership in a community include 1) commitment that involves responsibility, equality, and trust among persons who share a variety of gifts or resources; 2)common struggle and work involving risk, continuing growth, and hopefulness in moving toward a goal or purpose transcending the group itself; 3) contextuality in interacting with a wider community of persons, social structures, values and beliefs that may provide support and correctives. She contends there is never a complete equality in a dynamic relationship, but a pattern of equal regard and mutual acceptance among partners is essential.

The true community of Christians should have the center of focus in Jesus Christ. The community is not formed because of any particular superiority of the members. But the new focus of the relationship in Jesus Christ is setting persons free for others. The centrality of the new community should be to transcend human purposes, and unite to work for God's purpose and God's kingdom on earth which is yet to come.

The new community with new paradigm is a partnership with God as well as with individuals who share common goals in the relationship of the creation. But God chose to be a partner with a suffering humanity as Immanuel (Matt. 1:23) not to be served, but to serve. God invites us to be a partner of service with God and for God. God invites us to be a partner in freedom with God and for others. God invites us to be a partner with God for the future.

Conclusion: The Struggle for Justice

Efforts made in support of humanization of women in church can be seen in three parts: Biblical reinterpretation approach, liberation approach, and searching for a new paradigm. In striving to support partners in a new community, many church women's organization feel that the preparation and the work should be done through education, change of parliamentary policies, inclusive language and effective leadership training. Many are at work at reconstruction of women's own internalized image of being less than a human. Many are at work at the construction of women's own theology. Many are calling for economic justice for women in this capitalistic society.

Many seminaries have 30 to 51 percent women seminarians in their student body. Resource material on the issue of ordination of women are being used for implementation. Resource materials on inclusive language usage for worship, liturgy and hymns are ready for use. Many seminars and workshops are being planned to train church leaders, youth leaders and women leaders on administrative skills, and organizational and planning skills.

Many believe that the central nature of God's revelation about the church is that the church is the "whole people of God," sharing and supporting the real life experiences and being servants to one another. Humanity includes identity and community.

It would be a major advance if most of the Christian churches and institutions adopted a paradigm that would more adequately reflect the practice of Jesus and the first century church. It would even be better if the church would encourage and support everyone involved in their active commitment and ministries as a way of providing the hope for the future and as a way of practicing love of Christ for all who are on the pilgrimage together in this small world.

Reference

Bachofen, Johann Jakob. *Myth, Religion and Mother Rights: Selected Writings of J. J. Bachofen.* Princeton: Princeton University Press, 1967.

Christ, Carol P. and Judith Plaskow, eds. *Womanspirit Rising: A Feminist Reader in Religion.* New York: Harper and Row, 1979.

Cone, James H. *God of the Oppressed.* New York: Seabury, 1975.

Cornwell Collective. *Your Daughters Shall Prophesy.* New York: Pilgrim, 1980.

Daly, Mary. *Beyond God the Father: Toward a Philosophy of Women's Liberation.* Boston: Beacon, 1974.

Doeley, Sarah Bentley. *Women's Liberation and the Church: The New Demand for Freedom in the Life of the Christian Church.* New York: Association, 1970.

Fiorenza, Elisabeth Schüssler. *In Memory of Her: A Feminist Theological Reconstruction of Christian Origins.* New York: Crossroad, 1983.

Hageman, Alice, ed. *Sexist Religion and Women in the Church: No More Silence.* New York: Association, 1974.

Harrison, Beverly. *Making the Connections: Essays in Feminist Social Ethics*. Boston: Beacon, 1985.

Heyward, Isabel Carter. *The Redemption of God: Toward a Theology of Mutual Relation*. Washington, D.C.: University Press of America, 1982.

Inclusive Language Lectionary. Division of Education and Ministry, National Council of the Churches of Christ in the U.S.A. Atlanta: John Knox; New York: Pilgrim; Philadelphia: Westminster, 1983.

Jewett, Paul. *The Ordination of Women*. Erdmans, 1980.

Katoppo, Marianne. *Compassionate and Free: An Asian Woman's Theology*. Geneva: World Council of Churches, 1979.

Kim, Yung-Chung. *Women of Korea: A History from Ancient Times to 1945*. Seoul: Ewha Womans University Press, 1976.

MacDonald, Dennis r. "There Is No Male and Female: Galatians 3:26-28 and Gnostic Baptismal Tradition." Ph.D. Dissertation, Harvard University, 1978.

Neufer-Emswiler, Sharon and Thomas. *Women and Worship: A Guide to Non-Sexist Hymns, Prayers, and Liturgies*. New York: Harper and Row, 1974.

Nugent, Robert, ed. *The Challenge to Love*. New York: Crossroad, 1983.

Pagels, Elaine. "Paul and Women: A response to Recent Discussion." *Journal of the American Academy of Religion* 42 (1974) 538-49.

Parvey, Constance F., ed. *The Community of Women and Men in the Church—The Sheffield Report*. Philadelphia: Fortress, 1983.

Ruether, Rosemary R. *Religion and Sexism: Images of Woman in the Jewish and Christian Traditions*. New York: Simon and Schuster, 1974.

_____. *New Woman/New Earth: Sexist Ideologies and Human Liberation*. New York: Seabury, 1975.

_____. *Sexism and God-Talk: toward a Feminist Theology*. Scranton, PA: Harper and Row, 1983.

Russell, Letty M. *Human Liberation in a Feminist Perspective—A Theology*. Philadelphia: Westminster, 1974.

_____, ed. *The Liberating Word: A Guide to Non-Sexist Interpretation of the Bible*. Philadelphia: Westminster, 1976.

_____. *The Future of Partnership*. Philadelphia: Westminster, 1979.

————. *Becoming Human*. Philadelphia: Westminster, 1982.

Sakenfeld, Katharine D. "The Bible and Women: Bane or Blessing," *Theology Today* 32/3 (October 1975) 222-33.

Sargent, Alice G. *Beyond Sex Roles*. New York: West Publishing Co., 1977.

Sawicki, Marianne. *Faith and Sexism—Guidelines for Religious Educators*. New York: Seabury. 1979.

Scanzoni, Letha & Nancy Hardesty. *All We're Meant to be: A Biblical Approach to Women's Liberation*. Waco, Texas: Word Books, 1974.

Soelle, Dorothee. *Choosing Life*. Philadelphia: Fortress, 1981.

Stendahl, Krister. *The Bible and the Role of Women*. Philadelphia: Fortress, 1966.

Swidler, Leonard. *Biblical Affirmations of Woman*. Philadelphia: Westminster, 1979.

Swidler, Leonard. "Jesus Was a Feminist," *Southeast Asia Journal of Theology*, Vol. 13/1, 1972.

Thompson, Betty. *A Chance to Change: Women and Men in the Church*. Philadelphia: Fortress, 1982.

Trible, Phyllis. "Woman in the Old Testament," *Interpreter's Dictionary of the Bible*, Supplementary Volume. Nashville: Abingdon, 1976.

Ulanov, Ann. *Receiving Woman: Studies in the Psychology and Theology of the Feminine*. Philadelphia: Westminster, 1981.

Verdesi, Elizabeth. *In But Still Out: Women in the Church*. Philadelphia: Westminster, 1976.

Washbourn, Penelope. *Becoming Woman*. New York: Harper and Row, 1977.

Weidman, Judith L. ed. *Women Ministers: How Women are Redefining Traditional Roles*. New York: Harper and Row, 1981.

Wold, Margaret. *The Shalom Woman*. Minneapolis: Augsburg. 1975.

The Power of Anger
in the Work of Love:

Christian Ethics for Women
and Other Strangers

Beverly W. Harrison

Undoing Patriarchal Processions

Readers who are knowledgeable in feminist theology and who have had sufficient intellectual energy to read and appropriate Mary Daly's powerful, angry book *Gyn/Ecology: The Metaethics of Radical Feminism,* may already understand why it was important then, as now, to begin a discussion of feminist ethics by focusing on the issue of academic processions. Processions, Daly argues, exemplify all that is wrong with the patriarchal world; they are the essence of "the deception of the fathers."[1] Daly believes that this "deception of the fathers"—the way we were all taught to view the work through rigidly compartmentalized, static categories and academic disciplines—is killing us all. This fixation with processions, she contends, has its origins in Christianity, beginning with the procession of the trinitarian god. The god of Christian orthodoxy—with its threefold, exclusively male manifestation—

Reprint from Making the Connections with permission from the publisher, Beacon Press, Boston, Mass.

is, she suggests, expressive of the male homosexual fixation that underlies the dominant spirituality of our culture, whether in an ecclesiastical or an academic expression. In either academic or ecclesiastical contexts, processions mark out clearly, and protect, male privilege and control. Daly stresses that this sacralizing and deification of male functions in our world will be ended only if women who understand the idolatry involved give up participation in processions altogether. In fact, she is so serious in this claim that the power of procession sustains the patriarchal oppression of women that she designates "procession" as the *first* (the very first) of the eight deadly sins of Phallocracy.[2] These eight deadly sins represent Daly's alternative way of viewing human evil; they replace the traditional seven deadly sins of Christian teaching. It should not be lost on any of us that on the traditional list of deadly sins the "sin" of anger was usually given conspicuous emphasis. Happily, no feminist analysis could perpetuate the notion that anger, per se, is evil, and Daly's analysis surely does not do so.

I acknowledge that Mary Daly would not exempt even an academic procession numerically dominated by females from her unequivocal indictment of processions as instruments of patriarchy. She is adamant that processions can be only a "frozen mirror image" of "Spinning," which is her metaphor of the wholistic, spontaneous, intellectually imaginative modes of knowing, being, and doing on which women—when not dependent on patriarchy for doing of which women—when not dependent on patriarchy for self-definition—are capable. There can be no doubt that the mere presence of a *few* women in traditional processions serves, first and foremost, to disguise the devastation that dominant institutions wreak upon women and others who do not "fit in"—for example, males of color or males whose ideological viewpoint of sexual orientation does not reinforce the dominant cultural mode. Even so, my theory of social change obviously diverges from hers or I would not have organized a procession at all.

I agree with Daly that a chief evidence of patriarchal control in our world is women's subtle conditioning that reinforces our reluctance to develop a sense of our own power to identify, name, and characterize our world. For all of the methodological differences that separate my position from Daly's,[3] it is not part of my argument with her to deny the depth of the problem of misogyny in human history or in the dominant forms of historical Christianity. Among the many debts we owe Mary Daly is this: She has described the problem in an uncompromising way and has made it impossible for any intellectually honest person to deny the necessity of a feminist critique of Christianity. I have long argued this point in light of Daly's analysis—that it should never be the business of any feminist who remains within the Christian church must have, and has yet to have, with the full force of a feminist critique. We have very far to go before Christianity acknowledges adequately its complicity in breeding and perpetuating the hatred and fear of the real, full, lived-world power of female persons! Misogyny, as

Daly claims, is hydra-headed, having as many forms as there are cultures, languages, and social systems. She is right to insist that what is feared is not "femininity," that clever nineteenth-century invention, but the spooking, sparking power of *real* women who do not need to stand around waiting for male approval. Misogyny's real force arises only when women assert ourselves and own our power. Mark this point well: It is never the mere presence of a woman, nor the image of women, or fear of "femininity," that is the heart of misogyny. The core of misogyny, which has yet to be broken or even touched, is the reaction that occurs when women's concrete power is manifest, when we women live and act as full and adequate persons in our own right. Even when Daly's specific historical portrayal of misogyny is carelessly done,[4] she still has a firm sense of the *depth* of what must be undone in human life if the culturally diverse patterns of women-hating are to end. It would be a form of deep intellectual dishonesty not to acknowledge that only Mary Daly's profound rage has produced a feminist critique strong enough to assure that some minimal attention must be given it within ecclesiastical and academic circles.

At times I wish I believed, with Daly, that the power of patriarchy could be overthrown if only we women would absent ourselves from patriarchal processions altogether. If only the *withholding* of power were adequate to bring about social change in our world, undoing oppression would not be difficult. However, we women should be the last to allow

145

ourselves to be trapped in the "spiritualizing" notion that real change in our flesh and blood world ever comes from absenting ourselves from what is going on in that world. Only a few women are in a position even to fantasize such options of withdrawal. Hardly any of our foresisters had such an option.

Even if many contemporary women were to choose the option of nonparticipation, we may be sure that processions would continue precisely because they are such powerful human actions, which is to say that they express energy, movement, and festivity. If men have enjoyed them, why should women not enjoy them too? Like all powerful public rituals, all dramatic human activity, processions shape our sense of who we are as actors, or what in the language of ethics we call "moral agents." They shape not only what we call our "personal moral sense" or sense of identity and self-worth but also our sense of destiny and community—what we call our "moral ethos." They always have and they always will. Processions cannot be abandoned because we *all* live by a sense of plausibility and legitimacy that we gain from them. Be assured that whatever passes in our common life as sacred truth or profound wisdom has been and will always be shaped and celebrated through such occasions. So those excluded from processions in our flesh and blood world suffer very palpable loss, real injuries to dignity, real assaults on self-respect and sense of worth.

This is why I cannot concur with Daly's call to women to abandon processions and join the

"Journey to the Otherworld" of segregated feminism. The joyful world of Womanspace, which she commends to us as a permanent habitat, can be at best only an occasional sanctuary for the feminist *for whom life itself, and the embodied world of flesh and blood,* are the true gifts of God. For this reason the turn in Mary Daly's writing, marked by a new emphasis on the language of otherworldliness, disturbs me. In contrast to Daly, my basic ethical thesis is that women, and other marginated people, are *less* cut off from the real, material conditions of life than are those who enjoy the privileges of patriarchy and that, as a result, an otherworldly spirituality is far removed from the life experience of women. Even if Daly were clear, as I hope she is, that her use of the language of otherworldliness is metaphorical, her imagery still seems misguided. Our need is for a moral theology shaped and informed by women's actual historical struggle. Women's experience, I submit, could not possibly yield an "otherworldly" ethic. Nor can feminists ignore the growing but morally dubious fascination with forms of world-denying spirituality in our culture. In light of a massive trend toward escapist religiosity, Daly's imagery, even if it stems from poetic license, is dangerous. It gives aid and comfort to those who have very strong political and economic reasons to encourage a spirituality that does not focus on injustice and the personal suffering it generates. Feminists, whose commitments must be to deep and profound change, should have no part in supporting a world-denying spirituality or in encouraging ways of speaking about the world that may invite withdrawal from struggle.

"Otherworldliness" in religion has two very different sources in our social world of knowledge. One sort of otherworldly religion appears among the poor and downtrodden, reflecting a double dynamic in their experience: It reflects a hopelessness about this world that is engendered by living daily with the evil of oppression, but it also fuels and encourages an ongoing struggle against the present order by conjuring a better time and a better place, beyond the oppressive here and now. However, an entirely different form of otherworldliness appears amongst those of us who have never been marginated who have lived well above the daily struggle to survive, when our privileges are threatened. This form of otherworldliness is merely escapist, and its political consequences are entirely reactionary. Its result is to encourage denial of responsibility for the limited power that we do have, and it always results in reinforcing the status quo.

Daly's metaphorical leap into Otherworldly Womanspace may well come from the real agony and pain she has experienced in the face of misogyny.[5] The inexhaustibility of her rage suggests that this is so. However, a feminist metaethics must not fail to affirm and generate our power to affect the existing world. We must wrest this power of action from our very rightful anger at what has been done to us and to our sisters and to brothers who do not meet patriarchy's expectations. The deepest danger to our cause is that our anger will turn inward and lead us to portray ourselves and other women chiefly as victims rather than those who have struggled for the gift of life against incredible odds. The creative power of anger is shaped by owning this great strength of women and of others who have struggled for the full gift of life against structures of oppression.

We need not minimize the radicality of women's oppression in varied cultures and communities or minimize Christianity's continuing involvement in that oppression, but we must not let that recognition confirm us in a posture of victimization. Let us note and celebrate the fact that "woman-spirit rising" is a global phenomenon in our time. Everywhere women are on the move. Coming into view now, for the first time, on a worldwide scale, is the incredible *collective* power of women so that anyone who has eyes to see can glimpse the power and strength of women's full humanity. We dare not forget, in spite of the varied forms of women's historical bondage, that we have also been, *always*, bearers of many of the most precious and special arts of human survival. The Chinese revolutionary slogan "Women hold up half of the sky" is not mere hyperbole. In spite of a literary historical tradition that has ignored the fact, women always have held up half, or more than half, of the sky. This astonishing cross-culture phenomenon of women's rising consciousness going on all around us could not have happened if this deep human power of women were not already grounded reality. I submit that even the present widespread cultural and political backlash against feminism is strong testimony to this fact. To be sure, the full world historical project that feminism envisages remains a distant dream—that is, that every female child in *each* and *every* community and culture will be born to share a full horizon of human possibility, that she will have the same range of life options as every male child. This is, and remains, "the longest revolution." But this revolution, for which we have every right to yearn, will come sooner if we celebrate the strength that shines forth in women's lives. This strength and power must stand at the center of the moral theology that feminism generates.

What I propose to do in the space remaining is to identify several positive dimensions of women's historical experience that I believe are most urgent to the reshaping of traditional Christian theological ethics to bring that ethics closer to a moral norm inclusive of all humanity. I also invite you to consider what difference it would make to our understanding of "the greater commandment"—our love of God and our love of neighbor—if these basepoints drawn from women's experience received their due. It is out of such a process that we can begin to develop an adequate feminist moral theology.[6]

My basic thesis that a Christian moral theology must be answerable to what women have learned by struggling to lay hold of the gift of life, to receive it, to live deeply into it, to pass it on, cannot be fully defended here. My theological method is consonant with those other liberation theologies that contend that what is authentic in the history of faith arises only out of the crucible of human struggle.[7] This I take to be *the* central, albeit controversial, methodological claim of all emergent liberation theologies. That the locus of divine revelation is in the concrete struggles of groups and communities to lay hold of the gift of lift to unloose what denies life has astonishing implications for ethics. It means, among other things, that we must learn what we are to know of love from immersion in the struggle for justice. I believe that women have always been immersed in the struggle to create a flesh and blood community of love and justice and that we know much more of the radical work of love than does the dominant, otherworldly spirituality of Christianity. A feminist ethic, I submit, is deeply and profoundly worldly, a spirituality of sensuality.[8]

Basepoints for a Feminist Moral Theology

Activity as the Mode of Love

The first point at which women's experience challenges the dominant moral theology is difficult to see historically because of the smoke screen created by a successful nineteenth-century male counterattack on the first women's liberation movement. Because of this counterattack, most educated, middle-strata women have internalized an ideology about ourselves that contradicts our actual history. Historically, I believe, women have always exemplified the power of activity over passivity, of ex-

151

perimentation over routinization, of creativity and risk-taking over conventionality. Yet since the nineteeth century we have been taught to believe that women are, by nature, more passive and reactive than men. *If* women throughout human history have behaved as cautiously and as conventionally as the "good women" invented by late bourgeois spirituality, *if* women had acquiesced to "the cult of true womanhood," and *if* the social powerlessness of women that is the "ideal" among the European and American "leisure classess" had prevailed, the gift of human life would long since have faced extinction.

This is very modern invitation to us women to perceive ourselves under the images of effete gentility, passivity, and weakness blocks our capacity to develop a realistic sense of women's historical past. The fact is that while there are few constants in women's experience cross-culturally, the biological reality of childbearing and nursing (never to be confused with the cultural power of nurturance) usually gave women priority in, and responsibility for, those day-to-day activities that make for human survival in most societies. For example, women—not men— are the breadwinners and traders in many precapitalist societies. If we modern women acquiesce in the seductive invitation to think of ourselves primarily as onlookers, as contemplators, as those who stand aside while men get on with the serious business of running the (public) world, we should at least recognize what a modern "number" we are doing on ourselves! The important point here, however, is that a theology that overvalues static and passive

152

qualities as "holy," that equates spirituality with noninvolvement and contemplation, that views the activity of sustaining daily life as mundane and unimportant religiously, such as theology *could not have been formulated by women.* In contrast, Sojourner Truth spoke authentically, out of the real lived-world experience of women, when she defined her womanhood in this way:

Nobody ever helped me into carriages, or over mud puddles, or have me the best place. And ain't I a woman? Look at me! Look at my arm! I have ploughed and planted and gathered into barns, and no men could head me! And ain't I a woman? I can work as much and eat as much as any man when I can get it and bear the lash as well. And ain't I a woman? I have borne thirteen children and seen most of them sold off to slavery, and when I cried out with my mother's grief, none but Jesus heard me. And ain't I a woman?[9]

Women have been the doers of life-sustaining things, the "copers," those who have understood that the reception of the gift of life is not inert thing, that to receive this gift is to be engaged in its tending, constantly. I believe we have a very long way to go before the priority of activity over passivity is internalized in our theology and even farther to go before love, in our ethics, is understood to be a *mode of action.* In *Beyond God the Father*,[10] Mary Daly

153

began the necessary theological shift by insisting that a feminist theism has no place for a God understood as stasis and fixity, that out of women's experience the sacred is better imaged in terms of process and movement. Her proposal that God be envisaged as Be-ing, and verb rather than as noun, struck a deep chord in her readers, and not merely in her women readers.

Even so, Daly's reformulation does not seem to me even to go far enough. Susanne Langer has rightly noted that philosophies of being—those philosophies that take the structures of nature as their starting point—have long since incorporated the notion that process is the basic structure of reality. Process theologians rightly protest that Daly has not paid enough attention to, or given enough credit to, modern philosophy of religion for incorporating these new views of nature. However, not many process theologians—indeed, even Daly—recognize the further need to incorporate the full meaning of the human struggle for life into our understanding of God. It is necessary to open up the naturalistic metaphors for God to the power of human activity, to freedom not only as radical creativity but also as radical moral power. It is necessary to challenge the classic ontology of Be-ing even more deeply than Daly has done. Catholic natural law theologies, it has often been argued, fail to do justice to the fact that the power of nature passes through what Marx called "the species-being" of human nature. Our world and our faith are transformed, for good or ill, through human activity. A feminist moral theology

154

needs to root its analysis in this realm of radical moral creativity. Such freedom is often abused, but the power to create a world of moral relations is a fundamental aspect of human nature itself. In my opinion, the metaphor of Be-ing does not permit us to incorporate the radicality of human agency adequately. *Do-ing* must be as fundamental as *be-ing* in our theologies. Both do-ing and be-ing are only "ways of seeing things." However, we can never make sense of what is deepest, "wholiest," most powerfully sacred in the lives of women if we identify women only with the more static metaphor of being, neglecting the centrality of praxis as basic to women's experience. We women have a special reason to appreciate the radical freedom of the power of real, concrete deeds.

To be sure, some male-articulated "theologies of praxis" have given feminist theologians pause on this point. Men often envisage the power of human activity under images that suggest that domination and control are the central modes of human activity, as though political or military conquest were the noblest expressions of the human power to act. Because of this, some women have urged that feminist theologies eschew historical categories and operate exclusively from naturalistic metaphors. I believe that such a theological move would have disastrous consequences. We dare not minimize the very real historical power of women to be architects of what is most authentically human. We must not lose hold of the fact that we have been the chief builders of whatever human dignity and community

155

has come to expression. We have the right to speak of *building* human dignity and community.

Just as do-ing must be central to a feminist theology, so too be-ing and do-ing must never be treated as polarities. Receiving community as gift and doing the work of community building are two ways to view the same activity. A feminist theology is not a theology of either/or.[12] Anyone who has lived in "women's place" in human history has had to come to terms with the responsibility of being a reciprocal agent. Women's lives literally have been shaped by the power not only to bear human life at the biological level but to nurture life, which is a social and cultural power. Though our culture has come to disvalue women's role, and with it to disvalue nurturance, genuine nurturance is a formidable power.[13] Insofar as it has taken place in human history, it has been largely through women's action. For better or worse, women have had to face the reality that we have the power not only to create personal bonds between people but, more basically, to build up and deepen *personhood itself.* And to build up "the person" is also to deepen relationship, that is, to bring forth community.

We do not yet have a moral theology that teaches us the aweful, awe-some truth that we have the power through acts of love or lovelessness literally to create one another. I believe that an adequate feminist moral theology must call the tradition of Christian ethics to accountability for minimizing the deep power of human action in the work of or the denial of love. Because we do not understand love as

156

the power to act-each-other-into-well-being we also do not understand the depth of our power to thwart life and to maim each other. The fateful choice is ours, either to set free the power of God's love in the world or to deprive each other of the very basis of personhood and community. This power of human activity, so crucial to the divine-human drama, is not the power of world conquest or empire building, nor is it control of one person by another. We are *not* most godlike in our human power when we take the view from the top, the view of rulers, or of empires, or the view of patriarchs.

I believe that our world is on the verge of self-destruction and death because the society as a whole has so deeply neglected that which is most human and most valuable and the most basic of all the works of love—the work of human communication, of caring and nurturance, of tending the personal bonds of community. This activity has been seen as women's work and discounted as too mundane and undramatic, too distracting from the serious business of world rule. Those who have been taught to imagine themselves as world builders have been too busy with master plans to see that love's work *is* the deepening and extension of human relations. This urgent work of love is subtle but powerful. Through acts of love—what Nelle Morton has called "hearing each other to speech"[14]—we literally build up the power of personhood in one another. It is within the power of human love to build up dignity and self-respect in each other or to tear each other down. We are better at the latter than the former.

157

However, literally through acts of love directed to us, we become self-respecting and other-regarding persons, and we cannot be one without the other. If we lack self-respect we also become the sorts of people who can neither see nor hear each other.

We may wish, like children, that we did not have such awesome power for good or evil. But the fact is that we do. The power to receive and give love, or to withhold it—that is, to withhold the gift of life—is less dramatic, but every bit as awesome, as our technological power. It is tender power. And, as women are never likely to forget, the exercise of that power begins, and is rooted in *our bodies, ourselves.*[15]

Our Bodies, Ourselves as the Agents of Love

A second basepoint for feminist moral theology derives from celebrating "embodiment."[16] A moral theology must not only be rooted in a worldly spirituality but must aim at overcoming the body/mind split in our intellectual and social life at every level. Feminist historical theologian Rosemary Ruether and, more recently, a number of male theologians have begun to identify the many connections between this body/mind dualism and our negative attitudes toward women.[17] Ironically, no dimension of our Western intellectual heritage has been so distorted by body/mind dualism as has our moral theology and moral philosophy, which is why a feminist moral theology is so needed. A number of male theologians—notably my colleague Tom Driver[19]—have begun to reenvisage Christian theology that repudiates the mind/body split. However, fewer men in the field of Christian ethics have grasped the connection between body/mind dualism and the assumption many moral theologians make that we are most moral when most detached and disengaged from life-struggle.[19] Far too many Christian ethicists continue to imply that "disinterestedness" and "detachment" are basic preconditions for responsible moral action. And in the dominant ethical tradition, moral rationality too often is *disembodied* rationality.

If we begin, as feminists must, with "our bodies, ourselves," we recognize that all our knowledge, including our moral knowledge, is body-mediated knowledge. All knowledge is rooted in our sensuality. We know and value the world, *if* we know and value it, through our ability to touch, to hear, to see. *Perception* is foundational to *conception*. Ideas are dependent on our sensuality. Feeling is the basic bodily ingredient that mediates our connectedness to the world. When we cannot feel, literally, we lose our connection to the world. All power, including intellectual power, is rooted in feeling. If feelings are damaged or cut off, our power to image the world and act into it is destroyed and our rationality is impaired. But it is not merely the power to conceive the world that is lost. Our power to value the world gives way as well. If we are not perceptive in discerning our feelings, or if we do not know what we feel, we cannot be effective moral agents. This is why psychotherapy has to be understood as a very basic form of moral education. In the absence of feelings there is no rational ability to evaluate what is happening. Failure to live deeply in "our bodies, ourselves" destroys the possibility of moral relations between us.

These days there is much analysis of "loss of moral values" in our society. A feminist moral theology enables us to recognize that a major source of rising moral insensitivity derives from being out-of-touch with our bodies. Many people live so much in their heads that they no longer feel their connectedness to other living things. It is tragic that when religious people fear the loss of moral standards, they become *more* repressive about sex and sensuality. As a result they lose moral sensitivity and do the very thing they fear—they discredit moral relations through moralism. That is why the so-called "moral" majority is so dangerous.

By contrast, a feminist moral theology, rooted in embodiment, places great emphasis on "getting clear," on centering, on finding ways to enable us to stay connected to other people and to our natural environment.[20] Unless we value and respect feeling as the source of this mediation of the world, we lose this connection. To respect feeling is not, as some have suggested, to become subjectiv*istic*. To the contrary, subjectiv*ism* is not the result of placing too much emphasis on the body and/or feeling. Subjec-tiv*ism* and moral*ism* derive instead from evading feeling, from not integrating feeling deeply at the bodily level. This is not to suggest, however, that

160

feelings are an end in themselves. We should never seek feelings, least of all loving feelings. Furthermore, the command to love is not now and never was an order to *feel a certain way*. Nor does the command to love create the power to *feel* love, and it was never intended to do so. Action does that. Feelings deserve our respect for what they are. There are no "right" and "wrong" feelings. Moral quality is a property of acts, not feelings, and our feelings arise in action. The moral question is not "what do I feel?" but rather "what do I do with what I feel?" Because this is not understood, contemporary Christianity is impaled between a subjectivist and sentimental piety that results from fear of strong feeling, especially strong negative feeling, and an objectivist, wooden piety that suppresses feeling under pretentious conceptual detachment. A feminist moral theology welcomes feeling for what it is—the basic ingredient in our relational transaction with the world.

The importance of all this becomes clear when we stop to consider the relation of our acts of love to our anger. It is my thesis that we Christians have come very close to killing love precisely because we have understood anger to be a deadly sin. Anger is not the opposite of love. It is better understood as a feeling-signal that all is not well in our relation to other persons or groups or to the world around us. Anger is a mode of connectedness to others and it is always a vivid form of caring. To put the point another way: anger is—and always is—a sign of some resistance in ourselves to the moral quality of the social relations in which we are immersed.

161

Extreme and intense anger signals a deep reaction to the action upon us or toward others to whom we are related.

To grasp this point—that anger signals something amiss in relationship—is a critical first step in understanding the power of anger in the work of love. Where anger rises, there the energy to act is present. In anger, one's body-self is engaged, and the signal comes that something is amiss in relation. To be sure, anger—no more than any other set of feelings—does not lead automatically to wise or humane action. (It is part of the deeper work of ethics to help us move through all our feelings to adequate strategies of moral action.) We must never lose touch with the fact that all serious human moral activity, especially action for social change, takes its bearings from the rising power of human anger. Such anger is a signal that change is called for, that transformation in relation is required.

Can anyone doubt that the avoidance of anger in popular Christian piety, reinforced by a long tradition of fear of deep feeling in our body-denying Christian tradition, is a chief reason why the church is such a conservative, stodgy institution? I suggest, however, that while many of us actually hold out little hope for the moral renewal of the Christian church in our time, we are reluctant to face the cause of moral escap*ism* in the church—namely, the fear of feeling and, more specifically, fear of the power of anger. We need to recognize that where the evasion of feeling is widespread, anger does not go away or disappear. Rather, in interpersonal life it masks itself as boredom, ennui, low energy, or it expresses itself in passive-aggressive activity or in moralistic self-righteousness and blaming. Anger denied subverts community. Anger expressed directly is a mode of taking the other seriously, of caring. The important point is that where feeling is evaded, where anger is hidden or goes unattended, masking itself, there the power of love, the power to act, to deepen relation, atrophies and dies.

Martin Buber is right that direct hatred (and hatred is anger turned rigid, fixated, deadened) is closer to love than to the absence of feeling.[21] The group or person who confronts us in anger is demanding acknowledgment from us, asking for the recognition of their presence, their value. We have two basic options in such a situation. We can ignore, avoid, condemn, or blame. Or we can act to alter relationship toward reciprocity, beginning a real process of hearing and speaking to each other. A feminist moral theology, then, celebrates anger's rightful place within the work of love and recognizes its central place in divine and human life.

The final and most important basepoint for a feminist moral theology is the centrality of relationship.

As a feminist moral theology celebrates the power of our human praxis as an intrinsic aspect of the work of *God's* love, as it celebrates the reality that our moral-selves are body-selves who touch and see and hear each other into life, recognizing sensuality as fundamental to the work and power of love, so above all else a feminist moral theology insists that relationality is at the heart of all things.

I am perfectly aware that our current preoccupation with "human relations," with "skills of relationship" is such that some have declared that our modern concern for relationship is merely trendy and faddish. It is true that, like everything else in late capitalism, "relationship" becomes transformed into a commodity to be packaged and exchanged at a price. To speak of the primacy of relationship in feminist experience, and to speak of a theology of relation, however, is not to buy in on the latest capitalist fad. It is, above all, to insist on the deep, total sociality of all things. All things cohere in each other. Nothing living is self-contained; if there were such a thing as an unrelated individual, none of us would know it. The ecologists have recently reminded us of what nurturers always knew—that we are part of a web of life so intricate as to be beyond our comprehension.[22] Our life is part of a vast cosmic web, and no moral theology that fails to envisage reality in this way will be able to make sense of our lives or our actions today.

In a recent, powerful, and pioneering work that lays the groundwork for a feminist theology of relationship,[23] Carter Heyward has made clear how far traditional Christian theism has wandered from the central concern with relationality that characterized the faith of the Israelite community and that was so central to Jesus' ministry. She stresses that the basic images of God that emerged in patristic Christianity were devoid of relationship. By stressing that God is "being itself" or is "the wholly other," the Christian tradition implies that a lack of relatedness in God is the source of divine strength. And this image of divine nonrelatedness surely feeds images of self that lead us to value isolation and monadic autonomy. In our dominant theologies and intellectual traditions, do we not think of ourselves as most effective, most powerful as moral agents when we are most autonomous and most self-reliant, when we least need anyone else's help or support?

In a brilliant work entitled *About Possessions: The Self as Private Property,* philosopher John Wikse notes the connection of the metaphors of self we use with the property metaphors dominant in the socioeconomic order. To be a free person, to be a self in this society, now, means "to possess oneself." We actually think of real freedom as "self-possession." Self-reliance and freedom from dependence on others is everything. Wikse argues, most plausibly, that it is now difficult to tell the difference between the way this culture's "ideal person" is supposed to behave and the way we have traditionally viewed the behavior of those who are idiots or suffer madness. The idiot, we had always assumed, is one cut off from relationship, one who does not share common meaning. Now, however, we also see maturity as involving the same freedom from relatedness; *self-*relatedness is now so much the highest value that we speak as if "being at one with oneself" were a condition for relationship to others rather than a consequence of it. The hope that we can control our identity from within fulfills a dream that we can live "beyond vulnerability" to others.[25]

165

Not surprisingly, Wikse sees an intimate connection between these ideals and the way in which one "grows up male" in this society. Learning this script of so-called "authenticity as self-possession" means being a real man. He illustrates how he learned to "take it like a man," how he got the hand of "hold(ing) onto oneself":

> I was taught that a real man is a masked man; the Lone Ranger. If others could see beneath the mask of self-possession, if they could know you in your real needs, they might reject you; a real man should not have needs. As a heroic stranger, a man performs a misson of salvation; problems are their problems, needs are theirs, not one's own...I was...taught [in graduate school] that to succeed I must present a facade of invulnerability to other men, a performer immune to criticism and with no connection to the people with whom I work.[26]

I submit that a theological tradition that envisaged deity as autonomous and unrelated was bound over time to produce a humanism of the sort we have generated, with its vision of "Promethean man," the individual who may, if he chooses, enter into relationship. Where our image of transcendence is represented to us as unrelatedness, as freedom from reciprocity and mutuality, the experience of God as living presence grows cold and unreal. But even after such a God is long dead, the vision of the human historical agent as one who may, or may not,

166

choose relationship lingers with us.

Such notions of love as also linger in a world like this—whether they are images of divine or of Promethean human love—are images of heroic, grand gestures of self-possessed people. It is an image of patronizing love, the love of the strong for the weak, or, conversely, the sniveling gratitude of the weak toward those stronger who grants "favors."

Never mind that none of us wants, or has ever wanted or needed, transactions with this sort of love. Never mind that we all know—unless our sense of self has already been twisted almost beyond human recognition by sadism and brutality—that the love we need and want is deeply mutual love, love that has both the quality of a gift received and the quality of a gift given. The rhythm of a real, healing, and empowering love is take and give, give and take, free of the cloying inequality of one partner active and one partner passive.

I shudder to think how many times during my years of theological study I came upon a warning from a writer of Christian ethics not to confuse real, Christian love with "mere mutuality." One senses that persons who can think this way have yet to experience the power of love as a real pleasure of mutual vulnerability, the experience of truly being cared for or of actively caring for another. Mutual love, I submit, is love in its deepest radicality. It is so radical that many of us have not yet learned to bear it. To experience it, we must be open, we must be capable of giving and receiving. The tragedy is that a masculinist reified Christianity cannot help us learn to be such lovers.

To dig beneath this reified masculinist idolatry is also, I believe, to move toward a recovery of a New Testament ethos of faith. Can Jesus' active embodiment of love be illumined by this image of mutuality? I believe it can. Orthodox Christological interpretations imply that somehow the entire meaning of Jesus' life and work is to be found in his headlong race toward Golgotha, toward crucifixion—as if he sought suffering as an end in itself to complete the resolution of the divine human drama once and for all.[26] I believe that his way of viewing Jesus' work robs it of its—and his—moral radicality. Jesus was radical not in his lust for sacrifice but in his power of mutuality. Jesus' death on a cross, his sacrifice, was no abstract exercise in moral virtue. His death was the price he paid for refusing to abandon the radical activity of love—of expressing solidarity and reciprocity with the excluded ones in his community. Sacrifice, I submit, is not a central moral goal or virtue in the Christian life. Radical acts of love—expressing human solidarity and bringing mutual relationship to life—are the central virtues of the Christian moral life. That we have turned sacrifice into a moral virtue has deeply confused the Christian moral tradition.

Like Jesus, we are called to a radical activity of love, to a way of being in the world that deepens relation, embodies and extends community, passes on the gift of life. Like Jesus, we must live out this calling in a place and time where the distortions of loveless power stand in conflict with the power of love. We are called to confront, as Jesus did, that which thwarts the power of human personal and communal becoming, that which twists relationship, which denies human well-being, community, and human solidarity to so many in our world. To confront these things, and to stay on the path of confrontation, to break through the "lies, secrets and silences"[29] that mask the prevailing distortions and manipulations in relationship and the power of relations is the vocation of those who are Jesus' followers.

It is one thing to live out a commitment to mutuality and reciprocity as the way to bear up God in the world and to be clear-eyed and realistic about what the consequences of that radical love may be. It is quite another to do what many Christians have done—that is, to rip the crucifixion of Jesus out of its lived-world context in his total life and historical project and turn sacrifice into an abstract norm for the Christian life. To be sure, Jesus was faithful unto death. He stayed with his cause and he died for it. He *accepted sacrifice*. But his sacrifice was *for* the cause of radical love, to make relationship and to sustain it, and, above all, to *righting* wrong relationship, which is what we call "doing justice."

Needless to say, in the best of times and under the most propitious of circumstances, it is risky to live as if the commonwealth of the living God were present—that is, to live radical mutuality and reciprocity. Radical love creates dangerous precedents and lofty expectations among human beings. Those in power believe such love to be "unrealistic" because those touched by the power of such love tend to develop a reluctance to accept anything less than mutuality and self-respect, anything less than human dignity, anything less than authentic relatedness. It is for that reason that such persons become powerful threats to the status quo. As women have known, but also as men like Martin Luther King, Jr., and Archbishop Oscar Romero understood, as any must know who dare to act deeply and forcefully out of the power of love, radical love is a dangerous and serious business. Without blessed persistence, without the willingness to risk, even unto death, the power of radical love would not live on in our world. There are no ways around crucifixions, given the power of evil in the world. But as that poetic theologian of the gay liberation movement Sandra Browders has reminded us, the aim of love is not to perpetuate crucifixions, but to bring an end to them in a world where they go on and on and on! We do this through actions of mutuality and solidarity, not by aiming at an ethic of sacrifice.

Mark the point well: *We are not called to practice the virtue of sacrifice.* We are called to express, embody, share, celebrate the gift of life, and to pass it on! We are called to reach out, to deepen relationship, or to right wrong relations—those that deny, distort, or prevent human dignity from arising—as we recall each other into the power of personhood. We are called to journey this way, to stay in and with this radical power of love. When you do that for me, I am often overwhelmed by your generosity, and I may speak of the sacrifice you make for me. But we both need to be perfectly clear that you are not, thereby, practicing the viture of sacrifice on me. You are merely passing on the power of love, gifting me as others have gifted you, into that power to *do* radical love.

Conclusion

There is much more to be said about the envisionment of the work of radical love within a feminist moral theology that takes its signals from what is deepest and best in women's historical struggle. Certainly, more also needs to be said about the depth of sin and evil in the world. It is important to remember that a feminist moral theology is utopian, as all good theology is, in that it *envisages* a society, a world, cosmos, in which, as Jules Girardi puts it, there are "no excluded one."[30] But feminist theology is also mightily realistic, in that it takes with complete seriousness the radical freedom we human beings have for doing good or *evil*. Since we acknowledge that we have, literally, the power to person-each-other into love—that is, into relationship—we can also acknowledge our power to obliterate dignity, respect, care, and concern for humanity from our world. All of that *is* within our power.

Far more than we care to remember, though, the evil that we do lives on, after us. The radicality of our vision of love gains its urgency from that very knowledge. The prophets of Israel were right to insist, long ago, that the sins of the fathers (and the mothers) live on in us, corroding and destroying the power of relation. The evil that they have done, like the evil we do, must be undone. This is why our human moral task sometimes seems overwhelming. We live in a time when massive and accumulated injustice, acted out over time, encounters answer in the rising anger of those whose dignity and life are being threatened by collective patterns of privilege that have to be undone. In a world such as this, actively pursuing the works of love will often mean doing all we can to stop the crucifixions, resisting the evil as best we can, or mitigating the suffering of those who are the victims of our humanly disordered relations. In the midst of such a world, it is still within the power of love, which is the good news of God, to keep us in the knowledge that none of us were born only to die, that we were meant to have the gift of life, to know the power of relation and to pass it on.

A chief evidence of the grace of God—which always comes to us in, with, and through each other—is this power to struggle and to experience indignation. We should not make light of our power to rage against the dying of the light. It is the root of the power of love. So may it never be said of any of us feminist theologians that we merely stood by, ladylike, when that power of love was called for or that we sought refuge in an Otherworld when we were needed here and now, in the line of march.

After Mary Daly lectures—on those somewhat rare occasions when men are invited to attend—it often happens that the first questioner is a man who inquires, in a befuddled way, "What about men?

What does this mean for us?" Since I do not share Mary Daly's reverse Thomism[31]—that is, since I believe that the major differences between men's and women's behavior are rooted in culture and history rather than in a relatively fixed "nature"—I trust that my male readers will not at this point be suffering any confusion about what this essay means for them. It is not that it is wrong for any of us to ask: "What does all this mean for me?" That is a good question. But in a feminist moral theology, good questions are answered *by something we must do*. It is, I submit, urgent that men join women in doing feminist moral theology[32]—that is, acting to keep the power of relationship alive in our world—because men have more public power than women and because there is so much to be done.

But I do not wish to end on too sentimental a note about the relations of men and women in our world. Mary Daly had very good reasons for warning us women about the dangers of joining male-originated patriarchal processions. Since her diagnosis of the problem is so much on target, none of us must ever forget that, if we must join patriarchal processions in order to get on with the radical work of love, we had better be very sure that we invite a lot of our friends to come along.

Footnotes.

1. Mary Daly. *Gyn/Ecology: the Metaethics of Radical Feminism.* Boston: Beacon Press, 1978, p. 33ff. Mary Daly's work has rightly shaped most discussion and debate among women in theological and religious studies. Few if any male scholars seem to appreciate the importance of Daly's critique of Christian theology as exemplary patriarchy, perhaps because it is easier to ignore her claims than to offer a serious rejoinder. I have chosen to take public issue with Daly here not to give aid and comfort to those who think her work "too angry" and "too manhating," but because, with the publication of *Gyn/Ecology* Daly enters directly into "Meta-ethics," or a discussion of the foundations of particular moral claims. It will not do, as Rebecca Porper did in a review in this journal (*Union Seminary Quarterly Review.* XXXV, No. 1 and 2. Fall & Winter. 1979-1980, pp. 126-28.) simply to treat the book as "beyond academic categories." Many of Daly's complaints about "Methodolatry" in academia are on target, but she is also developing a substantive conceptual position herself, so her own method (i.e. operative assumptions and appeals for justification) deserve scrutiny. Daly worries a great deal about anti-intellectualism among women. It would be an exemplification of such anti-intellectualism among women. It would be an exemplification of such anti-intellectualism not to hold her accountable for the factual and moral claims she makes, or for her explicit or implicit methodological moves.

2. Ibid. Pp. 27-31.

3. My differences with Daly are numerous and beyond full classification here. Methodologically, I believe Daly has not repudiated adequately the extreme abstract rationalism of her Roman Catholic philosophical background, nor has she completed the shift from static ontic categories to the process categories she often celebrates. Carter Heyward is correct in claiming that Daly remains philosophically a subjective idealist. (Carter Heyward. "Speaking and Sparking; Building and Burning." *Christianity and Crisis.* Vol 39, No. 5, April 2, 1979, p. 69.) I assume a connection between subjective idealism and the body-mind dualism of the western tradition. The test of one's philosophical epistemology always becomes clear at the level of action. Idealism produces a critique of concepts, but it does not produce a *historically concrete* critique of institutions (i.e. collective practice) or an alternative *strategy for action.* Even when Daly is correct about the depth of misogyny, her historical analysis of it lacks concreteness, nuance and accuracy, and the book does not open the way to a strategy of change for a real, material world. It is not surprising that many begin to connect Daly's position with the ancient Gnostic movements, which in their developed form became dualistic.

4. As noted above, the quality of Daly's historical scholarship leaves much to be desired, especially in light of the growing amount of competent feminist

research available on some of the historical periods about which she writes. Daly seems unwilling to draw upon the work of distinguished women colleagues whose training is in historical scholarship and who are better able to do historical analysis. The record of women's oppression is powerful enough, when carefully reconstructed, to ground Daly's claims without recourse to casual and non-contextual historical judgments. Daly often rips historical materials out of their cultural context, as for example in condemning the practice of "African Genital Mutilation" without noting that male subincision rites are part of the same cultural practice, or in condemning *both sides* of the sometimes contradictory treatment women in the U.S. receive at the hands of gynecologists. The result of this has been that many of Daly's critics have dismissed her substantive claims because of easily disputable historical overgeneralization.

5. Ibid. p. 413ff.

6. I am assuming here that a "feminist moral theology" arises from the in-depth experience of women's struggle for life and from the consciousness which arises through that struggle to live and to maintain a culture which expresses our lives. Such experience produces a critique of dominant, male-articulated Christian and secular theological, philosophical and moral assumptions. I want to stress that for me *biological gender does not ground this point of view;* women's *historical* struggle for

life grounds it. I agree with Mary Daly that a feminist perspective—in this case a feminist moral theology—cannot assume the adequacy of any male notions of "reason" or "revelation." However, since I am philosophically a dialectical materialist I believe that critique of tradition *equals transformation of tradition*. The goal of a feminist moral theology, then, as Daly suggests, is to expose the death-dealing assumptions in the male-articulated tradition. However, contrary to Daly, I insist that women's culture has also been alive and concretely implicated in the real historical past of existing religious communities. The goal is to break the male monopoly on past and present *interpretation* so as to thereby *displace* Patriarchal (i.e. idolatrous) tradition with a humanly inclusive one.

7. I want to stress the similarity of hermeneutical assumptions made by feminists and by other liberation theologians even though many male-articulated liberation theologies often relish misogynist and masculinist idolatrous assumptions. (See, for example, Juan Luis Segundo. *The Liberation of Theology*. Maryknoll: Orbis Press, note 55, pp. 37-38. Segundo would reserve the term "Christian" for the male element in revelation.) From the standpoint of the method of feminist theology, it is well to remember that women are *not a minority*. This means that the liberation theologies of all communities and groups *must be transformed* by the experience of women in those groups. If the world survives at all, all theologies will be forced to feminist assumptions

177

since women are underclass within every historical group. However, this also means, as noted here, that the liberation of women is "the longest revolution."

8. Roman Catholic Theologian, Matthew Fox, has particularly stressed this theme of sensuality and spirituality. Happily, he notes the connection between feminist theology and the recovery of a spirituality of sensuality. Matthew Fox. *On Becoming A Musical Mystical Bear.* New York: Paulist Press, paperback edition, pp. IX-XXVI, 1972.) He pursues this theme in other books, most recently in *A Spirituality Named Compassion.* Minneapolis: Winston Press, 1979.

9. Sojourner Truth's speech was recorded in *History of The Women's Suffrage Movement, Vol. I.* Reprinted in Alice Rossi (ed.) *The Feminist Papers,* New York: Bantam Books, 1973, pp. 426-429.

10. Mary Daly. *Beyond God the Father.* Boston: Beacon Press, 1973, pp. 35ff and *passim.*

11. Susan Langer. *Mind: An Essay On Human Feeling.* Vol. 1. Langer traces in minute detail the evolution of organic structure from invariant process to motivated *act* as the major transition point between mind and the rest of nature.

12. Beverly Harrison. "Sexism and the Language of Christian Ethics." Paper circulated by the Faith and Order Commission. National Council of Churches.

13. The best available study of the values and virtues intrinsic to a feminist ethic, which also stresses this nurturance theme, is Eleanor Haney. "What Is Feminist Ethics: A Proposal For Continuing Discussion." *Journal of Religious Ethics*, Vol. 8, No. 1, 1980, pp. 115-124.

14. Nelle Morton. "The Rising of Women Consciousness in a Male Language Structure." *Andover Newton Quarterly*. Vol. 12, No. 4 (March 1972), pp. 177-190.

15. The phraseology is from The Boston Women's Health Collective's *Ourbodies/Ourselves*. New York: Simon and Schuster. 1973. This work has been one of the most powerful influences in transforming women's self-understanding during the past decade.

16. An important work which elaborates this theme is James B. Nelson. *Embodiment: An Approach to Sexuality and Christian Theology*. Augsburg Press, 1979.

17. See especially, Rosemary Ruether. *New Woman: New Earth*. Seabury Press, 1975.

18. See especially, Tom F. Driver. *Patterns of Grace. Human Experience As Word of God*. 1977. Recognition of the problem is also receiving attention in the works of theologians such as Charles Davis and Harvey Cox and, as noted above, Matthew Fox.

19. Happily, a few recent works by male colleagues in stress the importance of body and feeling in *moral epistemology* in a way consonant with my thesis here. Cf. James Nelson, op. cit. and Daniel Maquire, *The Moral Choice*. Doubleday, 1978.

20. Cf. Haney, op. cit. Also, Anne Kent Rush, *Getting Clear: Body Work For Women*. New York: Random House, 1972.

21. Martin Buber. *I And Thou*. New York: Charles Scribners' Sons, 1970. (Walter Kaufmann, translator). P. 67f.

22. See, for example, Barry Commoner. *The Closing Circle*. New York: Alfred A. Knopf, 1971.

23. Isabel Carter Heyward. *The Redemption of God. A Theology of Mutual Relation*. (Unpublished doctoral thesis. Union Theological Seminary, 1979.)

24. John R. Wikse. *About Possession: The Self As Private Property*. University Park: The Pennsylvania University Press, 1977.

25. Ibid. pp. 44 and 45.

26. Ibid. pp. 12 and 13.

27. A major source for the denigration of mutuality in Protestant Christian Ethics was Anders Nygren's study, *Agape and Eros*, Philadelphia: Westminster

Press, 1953. Among those who followed Nygren here was Reinhold Niebuhr. See Eugene Outha, *Agape: An Ethical Analysis*, New Haven: Yale University Press, 1972, pp. 7-92. An early critique of Nygren never adequately appropriated was Daniel Day Williams, *The Spirit and Forms of Love*. Roman Catholic writers have usually included a More positive role for mutuality in ethics than have Protestants but the critique of sacrifice proposed here is relevant to Roman Catholic writers.

28. Much of the closing section of this essay was omitted when it was originally delivered because of the press of time.

29. For an excellent critique of orthodox Christologies see Heyward, *op. cit.* Also Dorothee Solle, *Christ the Representative*. Philadelphia: Fortress Press, 1967 and *Political Theology*, Philadelphia: Fortress Press, 1974.

30. From Adrienne Rich, *Lies, Secrets and Silences*, New York: W. W. Norton, 1979.

31. Jules Girardi, "Class Struggle and the Excluded Ones." Translated from Spanish and circulated by New York Circus from *Amoe Christiane Y Lucha De Classes*. Sigueme: Spain, 1975.

32. Thomas Aquinas argued, following Aristotle, that male and female "natures" differed because biological structure difference. This two-natures'

idea runs deep in Christian Theology. Daly has, of course, reversed the traditional argument, making women alone expressive of full rationality. She continues the traditional dualism, however.

33. Within a liberation theology method, "thinking" or "reflection" is, of course, a moment *within* praxis. We "do" theology, which *includes* our naming, interpretation and analysis of our world, in the *process* of acting to change it in a life-giving direction.

Women and Christianity: A Selected Bibliography
by
Inn Sook Lee

1. Biblical Studies:

Anderson, Bernhard W. "The Lord Has Created Something New: A Stylistic Study of Jer. 31: 15-22." *Catholic Biblical Quarterly*, Oct. 1978.

Bird, Phyllis. "Images of Women in the Old Testament," in *Religion and Sexism*. Edited by Rosemary R. Ruether. New York: Simon and Schuster, 1974.

Brown, Raymond E., et al., eds. *Mary in the New Testament: A Collaborative Assessment by Protestant and Roman Catholic Scholars*. Philadelphia: Fortress, 1978.

Brown, Raymond E. "Roles of Women in the Fourth Gospel." *Theological Studies* 36 (1975) 688-99.

Cerling, C. E. Jr. "An Annotated Bibliography of the N.T. Teaching about Women." *Journal of the Evangelical Theological Society* 16 (1973) 47-53.

Fiorenza, Elisabeth Schüssler. *Eschatology of the New Testament*. New York: Harper & Row, 1977.

Fischer, James A. *God Said: Let There Be Woman: A Study of Biblical Women*. New York: Alba House, 1979.

MacDonald, Dennis R. "There is No Male and Female: Galatians 3:26-28 and Gnostic Baptismal Tradition." Ph.D. Dissertation, Harvard University, 1978.

MacDonald, Dennis R. "Virgins, Widows, and Paul in Second Century Asian Minor." *Society of Biblical Literature*. Seminar Papers, 1979 I, 169-184.

MacLeod, Catriona M.K. *The Bible and Women*. ANEW, Chicago: Thomas More, n.d. 17 issues.

Mollenkott, Virginia Ramey. *The Divine Feminine: The Biblical Imagery of God as Female*. New York: Crossroad, 1983.

Mollenkott, Virginia Ramey. *Women, Men and the Bible*. Nashville: Abingdon, 1977.

Moltmann-Wendel, Elisabeth. *The Woman Around Jesus*. New York: Crossroad, 1983.

Nolan, Albert. *Jesus Before Christianity: The Gospel of Liberation*. Capetown: David Philip, 1976.

Otwell, John H. *And Sarah Laughed: The Status of Women in the Old Testament*. Philadelphia: Westminster, 1977.

Pagels, Elaine. *The Gnostic Gospels*. New York: Random House, 1979.

Pagels, Elaine. "Paul and Women: A Response to Recent Discussion." *Journal of the American Academy of Religion* 42 (1974) 538-49.

Robinson, James M. "The Gospel of Mary." *The Nag Hammadi Library in English*. New York: Harper and Row, 1977.

Russel, Letty M., ed. *The Liberating Word: A Guide to Non-Sexist Interpretation of the Bible,* Philadelphia: Westminster, 1976.

Scanzoni, Letha & Hardesty, Nancy. *All We're Meant to Be: A Biblical Approach to Women's Liberation.* Waco, Texas: Word Books, 1974.

Scroggs, Robin. *Paul for a New Day.* Philadelphia: Fortress, 1977.

Scroggs, Robin. "Woman in the New Testament." *Interpreter's Dictionary of the Bible*. Supplementary Volume. Nashville: Abingdon, 1976.

Sakenfeld, Katharine D. "The Bible and Women: Bane or Blessing." *Theology Today* 32/3 (October 1975) 222-33.

Stendahl, Krister. *The Bible and the Role of Women.* Philadelphia: Fortress, 1966.

Swidler, Leonard. *Biblical Affirmations of Woman*. Philadelphia: Westminster, 1979.

Tolbert, Mary Ann, ed. *The Bible and Feminist Hermeneutics*. Scholars Press, 1983.

Trible, Phyllis. "Depatriarchalizing in Bible Interpretation." *Journal of the American Academy of Religion*, 41 (1973).

Trible, Phyllis. "Woman in the Old Testament." *Interpreter's Dictionary of the Bible*, Supplementary Volume. Nashville: Abingdon, 1976.

Wahlberg, Rachel Conrad. *Jesus and the Free Woman*. New York: Paulist, 1978.

2. Theology, Philosophy and Ethics: Feminist Theology.

Brown, Robert McAfee. *Theology in a New Key*. Philadelphia: Westminster, 1978.

Brueggemann, Walter. "Israel's Social Criticism and Yahweh's Sexuality." *Journal of the American Academy of Religion* 45/3 Supplementary Volume, (Sept. 1977) 739-72.

Brooten, Bernadett. "Junia.....Outstanding Among the Apostles." *Women Priests*. Editied by Leonard and Arlene Swidler. New York: Paulist, 1977. 141-44.

Christ, Carol P. *Diving Deep and Surfacing: Women Writers on Spiritual Quest.* Boston: Beacon, 1980.

Christ, Carol P., & Plaskow, Judith, eds. *Womanspirit Rising: A Feminist Reader in Religion.* New York: Harper and Row, 1979.

Clark, Elizabeth & Richardson, Herbert, eds. *Women and Religion: A Feminist Sourcebook of Christian Thought.* New York: Harper and Row, 1977.

Collins, Sheila. *A Different Heaven and Earth: A Feminist Perspective on Religion.* Valley Forge, PA: Judson, 1974.

Cone, James H. *God of the Oppressed.* New York: Seabury, 1975.

Daly, Mary. *Beyond God the Father: Toward a Philosophy of Women's Liberation.* Boston: Beacon, 1974.

Devaney, Sheila Greeve, ed. *Feminism and Process Thought.* The Harvard Divinity School/Claremont Center for Process Studies Symposium Papers. New York: Edwin Mellen, 1981.

Engelsman, Joan Chamberlain. *The Feminine Dimension of the Divine*. Philadelphia: Westminster, 1979.

Fiorenza, Elisabeth Schüssler. *In Memory of Her: A Feminist Theological Reconstruction of Christian Origins*, New York: Crossroad, 1983.

Harrison, Beverly Wildung. *The Freedom of Choice*. Boston: Beacon Press, 1983.

_____. *Making the Connections: Essays in Feminist Social Ethics*. Boston: Beacon Press, 1985.

Heyward, Isabel Carter. *The Redemption of God: Toward a Theology of Mutual Relation*. Washington, D.C.: University Press of America, 1982.

_____. *Theology of Human Relationships*. Washington, D.C.: University Press of America, 1982.

Moltmann-Wendel, Elisabeth. *Liberty, Equality, Sisterhood*. Philadelphia: Fortress, 1978.

Nelson, James B. *Embodiment: An Approach to Sexuality and Christian Theology*. Minneapolis: Augsburg Press, 1978.

Pellauer, Mary. "Violence Against Women: The Theological Dimension." *Christianity and Crisis*, May 30, 1983, pp. 206-12.

Plaskow, Judith. "The Feminist Transformation of Theology." *Beyond Androcentrism: New Essays on Women and Religion.* Edited by Rita M. Gross. Scholars (for American Academy of Religion), 1977.

_____. *Sex, Sin, and Grace: Womens Experience and the Theologies of Reinhold Niebuhr and Paul Tillich.* Washington, D.C.: University Press of America, 1980.

Ruether, Rosemary R. *Religion and Sexism: Images of Woman in the Jewish and Christian Traditions.* New York: Simon and Schuster, 1974.

_____. *New Woman/New Earth: Sexist Ideologies and Human Liberation.* Seabury, 1975.

_____. *Mary: The Feminine Face of the Church.* Philadelphia: Westminster, 1977.

_____. *To Change the World: Christology and Cultural Criticism.* New York: Crossroad, 1981.

_____. *Sexism and God-Talk: Toward a Feminist Theology.* Scranton, PA: Harper and Row, 1983.

Russel, Letty M. *Human Liberation in a Feminist Perspective—a Theology*. Philadelphia: Westminster, 1974.

_____. *The Future of Partnership*. Philadelphia: Westminster, 1979.

_____. *Growth in Partnership*. Philadelphia: Westminster, 1981.

_____. *Becoming Human*. Philadelphia: Westminster, 1982.

Soelle, Dorothee. *Choosing Life*. Philadelphia: Fortress, 1981.

Swidler, Leonard. "Jesus Was a Feminist." *Southeast Asia Journal of Theology*, Vol. 13/1, 1972.

Trible Phyllis. *God and the Rhetoric of Sexuality*. Philadelphia: Fortress, 1978.

Ulanov, Ann. *Receiving Woman: Studies in the Psychology and Theology of the Feminine*. Philadelphia: Westminster, 1981.

Washbourn, Penelope. *Becoming Woman*. New York: Harper and Row, 1977.

Williams, Jar G. "Yahweh, Women, and the Trinity." *Theology Today*, 32 (1975-76).

Wold, Margaret. *The Shalom Woman*. Minneapolis: Augsburg. 1975.

3. Worship, Ministry, and Liturgy:

Achtemeier, Elizabeth. *Creative Preaching*. Nashville: Abingdon, 1980.

Bernadin, Joseph L. "The Ordination of Women." *Commonweal*, Vol. 103:2 January 1976 pp. 42-44.

Brooten, Bernadett J. *Women Leaders in the Ancient Synagogue*. Chico, CA: Scholars, 1982.

Burke, Mary P. *Reaching for Justice*. Center of Concern, 1980.

Clarke, Linda, et al. *Image Breaking/Image Building: A Handbook, for Creative Worship with Women of Christian Tradition*. New York: Pilgrim Press, 1981.

Cornwall Collective. *Your Daughters Shall Prophesy*. New York: Pilgrim Press, 1980.

Crotwell, Helen Gray. *Women and the Word: Sermons.* Philadelphia: Fortress, 1978.

Doeley, Sarah Bentley. *Women's Liberation and the Church: The New Demand for Freedom in the Life of the Christian Church.* New York: Association Press, 1970.

Durka, Gloria & Smith, Joanmarie, eds. *Aesthetic Dimensions of Religious Education.* New York: Paulist Press, 1979.

Elizondo, Virgil & Greinacher, Norbert. *Women in a Men's Church.* Seabury, 1980.

Gonzalez, Justo & Catherine. *Liberation Preaching.* Nashville: Abingdon, 1980.

Hageman, Alice, ed. *Sexist Religion and Women in the Church: No More Silence.* New York: Association Press, 1974.

Harris, Maria, *The D.R.E. (Director of Religious Education) Book.* New York: Paulist, 1976.

Heyward, Carter. *A Priest Forever: Formation of a Woman and a Priest.* New York: Harper and Row, 1976.

Hull, Gloria, Scott, P., & Smith, B. *But Some of Us Are Brave.* Feminist Press, 1981.

Inclusive Language Lectionary. Division of Education and Ministry, National Council of the Churches of Christ in the U.S.A. Atlanta: John Knox; New York: Pilgrim; Philadelphia: Westminster, 1983.

Jeremias, Joachim. "Appendix: The Social Position of Women." *Jerusalem in the Time of Jesus.* Philadelphia: Fortress, 1969.

Jewett, Paul. *The Ordination of Women.* Eerdmans, 1980.

McFague, Sallie. *Metaphorical Theology: Models of God in Religious Language.* Philadelphia: Fortress, 1982.

Neufer-Emswiler, Sharon & Thomas. *Women and Worship: A Guide to Non-Sexist Hymns, Prayers, and Liturgies.* New York: Harper and Row, 1974.

Nugent, Robert, ed. *The Challenge to Love.* New York: Crossroad, 1983.

Ohanneson, Joan. Woman: *Survivor in the Church.* Minneapolis, MN: Winston Press, 1980.

Parvey, Constance F., ed. *The Community of Women and Men in the Church—The Sheffield Report.* Philadelphia: Fortress, 1983.

_____. *Ordination of Women in Ecumenical Perspective*. Geneva: World Council of Churches, 1980.

Pilgrim Press Editors. *Spinning a Sacred Yarn: Women Speak from the Pulpit*. New York: Pilgrim Press, 1982.

Sargent, Alice G. *Beyond Sex Roles*. West Publishing Co., 1977.

Sawicki, Marianne. *Faith and Sexism—Guidelines for Religious Educators*, Seabury. 1979.

Verdesi, Elizabeth. *In But Still Out: Women in the Church*. Philadelphia: Westminster, 1976.

Watkins, Keith. *Faithful and Fair: Transcending Sexist Language in Worship*. Nashville: Abingdon, 1981.

Weidman, Judith L. ed. *Women Ministers: How Women are Redefining Traditional Roles*. New York: Harper and Row, 1981.

_____. ed. *Christian Feminism: Visions of a New Humanity*. New York: Harper and Row, 1984.

Zikmund, Barbara Brown, *Discovering the Church*. Philadelphia: Westminster, 1982.

4. History of Christianity:

Atkinson, Clarissa. *Mystic and Pilgrim: the Book and the World of Margery Kempe.* Ithaca, NY: Cornell University Press, 1983.

Clark, Elizabeth. *Women in the Early Church.* Wilmington, DL: Michael Glazier, 1983.

Cott, Nancy F. *The Bonds of Womanhood: Women's Sphere in New England, 1780-1835.* New Haven, CT: Yale University Press, 1977.

Douglas, Ann. *The Feminization of American Culture.* New York: Alfred A. Knopf, Inc., 1977.

Gies, Frances and Joseph. *Women in the Middle Ages.* New York: 1978.

Gottwald, Norman K. *The Tribes of Yahweh: A Sociology of the Religion of Liberated Israel, 1250-1050 B.C.* Maryknoll, NY: Orbis Press, 1979.

Irwin, Joyce. *Womanhood in Radical Protestantism, 1525-1675.* B. J. Duculot, 1972.

Ruether, Rosemary Radford, & McLaughlin, Eleanor, eds. *Women of Spirit: Female Leadership in the Jewish and Christian Traditions.* New York: Simon and Schuster, 1979.

Ruether, Rosemary Radford, & Keller, Rosemary Skinner, eds. *Women and Religion in America,* Vol. I The Nineteenth Century: A Documentary History. San Francisco: Harper and Row, 1981.

_____. *Women and Religion in America,* Vol. II. New York: Harper and Row, 1983.

5. Women of Color:

Buvinic, Mayra, ed. *Women and Poverty in the Third World.* Baltimore: Johns Hopkins University Press, 1983.

Falk, Nancy A., & Gross, Rita M., eds. *Unspoken Worlds: Women's Religious Lives in Non-Western Cultures.* New York: Harper and Row, 1980.

Hooks, Bell. *Ain't I a Woman: Black Women and Feminism.* Boston, MA: South End, 1981.

Humez, Jean McMahon, ed. *Gifts of Power: The Writings of Rebecca Jackson, Black Visionary, Shaker Eldress.* Amherst, MA: University of Massachusetts Press, 1981.

Hurston, Zora Neale. *The Sanctified Church.* Berkeley: Turtle Island, 1981.

Katoppo, Marianne. *Compassionate and Free: An Asian Woman's Theology.* Geneva: World Council of Churches, 1979.

Lindsay, Beverly, ed. *Comparative Perspectives of Third World Women: The Impact of Race, Sex, and Class.* Praeger Publishers, 1980.

Loewenberg, Bert James, & Bogin, Ruth, eds. *Black Women in Nineteenth Century American Life: Their Words, Thier Thoughts, Their Feelings.* Pennsylvania State University Press, 1976.

Moraga, Cherrie & Anzaldua, Gloria, eds. *This Bridge Called My Back: Writings by Radical Women of Color.* Watertown, MA: Persephone, 1981.

Niethammer, Carolyn. *Daughters of the Earth: The Lives and Legends of American Indian Women.* New York: Collier, 1977.

Smith, Barbara. *Home Girls: A Black Feminist Anthology.* Brooklyn, NY: Kitchen Table: Women of Color Press, 1983.

Wilmore, Gayraud & Cone, James H. *Black Theology: A Documentary History, 1966-1979.* New York: Orbis, 1979.

6. Mythology and Spirituality:

Davies, Stevan. *The Revolt of the Widows: The Social World of the Apocryphal Acts.* Carbondale: Southern Illinois University Press, 1980.

Downing, Christine. *The Goddess: Mythological Images of the Feminine.* New York: Crossroad, 1981.

Porterfield, Amanda. *Feminine Spirituality in America.* Philadelphia: Temple University Press, 1980.

—————————, *Lost Goddesses of Early Greece: A Collection of Pre-Hellenic Mythology.* Boston: Beacon, 1981.

Spretnak, Charlene, ed. *The Politics of Women's Spirituality: Essays on the Rise of Spiritual Power Within the Feminist Movement.* New York: Anchor/ Doubleday, 1981.

Weigle, Marta. *Spiders and Spinsters: Women and Mythology.* University of New Mexico Press, 1982.

7. Other Resources in Related Fields.

Asian Women's Journal. *Asian Women*. Asian-American Studies Center. Berkeley: University of California Press, 1975.

Bates, Ulku U. etal. *Women's Realties, Women's Choices: An Introduction to Women's Studies*. Hunter College Women's Studies Collective. New York: Oxford University Press, 1983.

Boston Women's Health Book Collective, *Our Bodies, Ourselves*. New York: Simon and Schuster, 1975.

Bulkin, Elly and Smith, Barbara. *Feminist Perspectives on Anti-Semitism and Racism: Two Essays*. Brooklyn, NY: Long Haul, 1983.

Chordorow, Nancy. *The Reproduction of Mothering: Psychoanalysis and the Sociology of Gender*. Berkeley: University of California Press, 1978.

Coward, Rosalind. *Patriarchal Precedents: Sexuality and Social Relations*. Boston: Pandora, 1983.

Degler, Carl N. *At Odds: Women and the Family in America from the Revolution to the Present*. Oxford, 1980.

199

Fernea, Elizabeth Warnock & Bezirgan, Basima Qattan, eds. *Middle Eastern Women Speak*. Austin TX: University of Texas Press, 1977.

Freeman, Jo. *The Politics of Women's Liberation*. David McKay, 1975.

Friday, Nancy. *My Mother/MySelf: the Daughter's Search for Identity*. New York: Dell, 1977.

Glennon, Lynda M., *Women and Dualism: A Sociology of Knowledge Analysis*. New York: Longman and Green, 1979.

Gilligan, Carol. *In A Different Voice: Psychological Theory and Women's Development*. Cambridge, MA: Harvard University Press, 1982.

Melville, M. *Twice a Minority*. Mosby, 1980.

Miller, Jean Baker. *Toward A New Psychology of Women*. Boston: Beacon, 1976.

Paul, Diana. *Women in Buddhism*. Berkeley: Asian Humanities Press. 1979.

Rigney, Barbara. *Lilith's Daughters: Women and Religion in Contemporary Fiction*. Madison, WI: University of Wisconsin Press, 1982.

Roy, Maria, ed. *Battered Women: A Psycho-sociological Study of Domestic Violence.* Van Nostrand Reinhold, 1977.

Ruether, Rosemary R. "Home and Work: Women's Roles and the Transformation of Values," in *Woman: New Dimensions. Edited Walter Burkhardt. Paulist, 1975.*

Schaef, Anne. *Women's Reality: An Emerging Female System in the White Male Society.* Winston, 1981.

Stellman, Jeanne Mager. *Women's Work, Women's Health: Myths and Realities.* New York: Random House, 1977.

Tuchman, Barbara. *A Distant Mirror.* Knopf, 1978.

Vanek, Joann. "Time Spent in Housework," in *The Economics of Women and Men.* Edited by Alice Amsden. New York: St. Martin's Press, 1980.

Walker, Alice. *The Color Purple.* New York: Harcourt Brace Jovanovich, 1982.

Welter, Barbara. *Dimity Convictions: The American Woman in the Nineteenth Century.* Ohio University Press, 1976.

www.ingramcontent.com/pod-product-compliance
Lightning Source LLC
Chambersburg PA
CBHW061731270326
41928CB00011B/2194